THIS BOOK IS FOR YOU

If you identify as being introverted, regardless of whether or not you have taken a personality test, this book is for you. If you recognise that when you are in high-energy, social environments, after a while you feel drained, then this book is for you. If you find that you like to think and reflect before speaking, as opposed to speaking the first thing that comes into your mind, this book is for you. If you are energised from spending time alone, or any of the other typical preferences associated with introverts, then this book is for you. If you have been led to believe that because of your introverted nature you aren't good enough or that there is something wrong with you or other self-limiting beliefs, as well as what I have described above, then this book is most definitely for you.

If you are an introverted woman who wants to be visible in what you do, and wants to lead with influence and impact, without having to change who you are, this book is a guide that will help you to achieve this.

If you lead or coach introverted women, it will give you an insight into the challenges they face and how you can support them to overcome those challenges. It will also help to increase your awareness of the unfavourable bias that exists towards introverts in the workplace.

QUIETLY VISIBLE: LEADING WITH INFLUENCE AND IMPACT REVIEWS

"Carol speaks with gravitas and great compassion about the challenges of introversion, and how to overcome them as someone who has walked the walk and now quite literally talks the talk! Carol offers her expertise to help others to challenge their limiting beliefs and ways of being towards fully embracing introversion as a hidden superpower!

The book sets itself apart from others on the topic of introversion by not only raising awareness of key issues such as self-doubt, self-promotion, to all too familiar traits of perfectionism and imposter syndrome. It goes further. Carol provides purposeful and step-by-step exercises on helping introverts to step towards greater fulfilment in their own skin...akin to a self-help book with wings as she draws on her own lived experience interwoven thorough the pages of the book!"

Sasi Panchal M.A., PMP (APM)

"What makes this book unique is the vulnerability that transpires through the personal stories and the examples of the clients. The exercises make it a powerful tool too for self-coaching and also for coaches to use with their clients. It opens a whole new world of possibilities by pushing away the binary view we typically have of introverts/extroverts. Introverts are more than shy, they are strong...in their ways. This book is also to be recommended to those who are extroverts to raise awareness and acceptance. When I read the book, I started to notice all senior executives and leaders who seem to be introverts and extroverts. I found that the majority of the Senior execs in my department were introverts! I was delighted as I see myself as an introvert but it gave me hope and opened even more avenues. I am sure this book will do the same for many others

I also like the fact the different chapters can be read independently and this book can be used as an everyday guide which we can refer to, to remind us of the truth about ourselves."

Dienaba Fofana, Principal Auditor

"Carol Stewart has written an invaluable book on raising your visibility for introverted leaders who are female. These highly talented women are often overlooked; and Carol provides plenty of ideas to empower this group of women to ensure they are visible and truly valued. This is a book to read if you want new ideas for being noticed more when you are naturally introverted, and I have no hesitation in recommending it."

Susan Heaton-Wright, Superstar Communicator

"Like the author of this book, I too am an introvert. Unlike the author and the majority of introverted women, who will undoubtedly choose this book for their own personal growth, I did not climb the corporate career ladder. I made a conscious decision in my thirties that that was something I did not want to do, but on reading through the book, I found myself nodding as I remembered situations in which my 'voice' was overlooked in my younger years, because I worked hard and quietly in the background believing that this was all you needed to do to 'get noticed and recognised'. And yet, this book is for me too, particularly the chapters on Positioning, Quiet Presence and Quiet Influence, because very shortly I will be to leaving the corporate world and as I enter the latter years of my midlife journey, I have accepted to myself that as an introverted woman, I want to be more visible in what I do and to be able to lead, support and guide others in a more influential and impactful manner in my own personal growth and holistic therapies business.

There is a lot to this book; it is not one that you can read easily and lightly in one evening. It is very thorough and will make you think deeply about your own personal situation. It may even make you feel uncomfortable or sad as you identify and resonate with some of the experiences of the author and the women she has coached. As you work through the many chapters, Carol Stewart has provided exercises and self-reflection questions for you to complete – ignore them at your own peril. If you are an introverted woman who wants to be visible in what you do, and/or want to lead with influence and impact without having to change who you are, this exceptional book is definitely for you!"

Valerie Lewis, Visualise and Bloom

"If you're an introverted woman leader seeking increased self-understanding and practical tried and tested solutions for overcoming barriers created by an extrovert-loving world, this book is for you. It really is a life changer. And a must-read for those introverted women who wish to succeed at work."

Claudia Crawley, CEO, Winning Pathways Coaching

"In an era, where visibility and high-energy traits are rewarded and the contribution of quiet leaders are not 'seen' let alone rewarded, *Quietly Visible* is timely. Supported by research and experience of the author, it debunks some of the stereotypes and the unconscious bias towards introverts. It also walks the reader through various exercises to help those who might see themselves as introverted leaders find ways of navigating through the maze of noisy environments with examples of how to lead with impact. This book speaks really to all of us, who need that space to think with clarity and to build our mental agility to work through the fast-paced world we live in. Amazing work, Carol. Thank you for this gift!"

Lily Naadu Mensah,
Personal Brand Strategist & author of Work Your QUIRKS

"*Quietly Visible: How to Lead with Influence and Impact as an Introverted Woman* is a must-have for women who believed they are destined to lead but who are natural introverts.

Well-written, easy to read and full of digestible facts, *Quietly Visible* is filled with tips that female introverts can use so that they can rise up the promotional ladder and get leadership roles without comprising who they are.

This debut book from award winning executive coach Carol Stewart lets the world know that introverted women can and do rock the world, and make an impact, but they do so more quietly than their extrovert counterparts."

Marcia Dixon, Award winning PR Specialist,
Speaker and Events Organiser

ABOUT THE AUTHOR

Known as The Coach for High Achieving Introverted Women, Carol Stewart is an Executive, Career and Business Coach and founder of Abounding Solutions, with over 25 years' coaching and leadership experience. She helps women (with a particular emphasis on introverted women) to be great leaders and to lead with influence and impact. She also provides workshops, training and talks to corporate gender networks and BAME (Black, Asian and Ethnic Minority) networks on career development, personal development, and leadership development, and she is a leadership team facilitator.

She has provided coaching, training and talks to organisations such as Royal Bank of Scotland, Barclays, Asurion, Department of Health, NHS England, National Association of African Americans in Human Resources (NAAAHR), Westminster City Council, Crown Prosecution Service, Metropolitan Police Service, London Borough of Croydon, London Borough of Waltham Forest, London Borough of Lambeth and more, as well as coaching private clients.

Carol was named as one of Britain's Top 50 Business Advisers in 2015 by Enterprise Nation, a LinkedIn Top Voice UK in 2017, 2018 and 2019, a We Are The City Rising Star Champion in 2018 for her work helping women to develop in their careers, and she was listed as one of Britain's most influential Black Christian women in 2019 by Keep the Faith Magazine.

Prior to starting her coaching business, Carol worked for the Ministry of Justice. Starting in one of the most junior roles, she progressed to a senior role with responsibility for the operation of a group of magistrates' courts where she was also a member of the Local Criminal Justice Board for four London boroughs.

Carol is a semi-regular columnist for the Sheffield Telegraph, a weekly newspaper established in 1855, and has also written for several other publications. She volunteers her time mentoring women business owners in developing countries for the Cherie Blair Foundation, volunteers for the Kreative Culture Club, a youth charity that provides services to help develop young people in the local community (having previously been Chair of the Board of Trustees), she is a school governor, and leads the Marketplace Ministry at her church.

Please see this link for further information about Carol's work: https://aboundingsolutions.com/

ACKNOWLEDGEMENTS

There are many people I want to thank, not just for their support with writing this book, but also for their support on this journey that has led me to where I am today.

First and foremost, my parents Bernice and Lindan Lewis, who helped shape the values of which I hold dear. My siblings, Valerie, Pat, Michael, Maxine and Simon; without your love and support over the years, I wouldn't have become the woman I've become.

To my son Jevanni; raising you was the most rewarding 'job' I've ever done. And whilst you thought I was the one teaching you, I also learnt, and continue to learn, a lot from you.

To my wonderful husband Simon; thank you for being so caring and supportive.

To my dear friend Jacqueline Clarke; thank you for always being there and for telling it to me as it is. I hope me taking my manuscript to read and edit on our annual girls' holiday this year didn't put a damper on it for you.

To Claudia Crawley, Sepi Roshan, Cherron Inko-Tariah, Hira Ali, Tash Pennant, Susan Heaton-Wright,

Mary Waring, Sara Hutchinson. When you run a business on your own, it's essential to have a support network, and you have all been a great support to me and my business over the years.

Thank you to Desireé Harris-Bonner for designing a cover that captures the essence of what this book is about and who it is for so brilliantly. The only brief I gave her was that it had to represent women of all nationalities who are quietly visible.

Thank you to Olivia, Zara and the rest of the Filament team, for bringing my book to life.

To my prayer partner Marcia Dixon; thank you for praying with me about this book for the past two years since it was just a thought.

To Sonia Brown MBE, my mentor; thank you for the tough love. Although painful at the time, it was just what I needed.

To Vanessa Vallely OBE; thank you for giving me the opportunity to blog for We Are The City, the first platform I blogged on. That opportunity helped me develop confidence in my writing ability.

Thank you to LinkedIn for providing the platform where I developed my authentic writing voice, which really took off once the publishing platform was opened up.

To my lovely clients and everyone who has shared their experience with me; your stories have inspired me to write and helped the book to come alive.

And last but by no means least, to God who gets all the glory.

I never used to consider myself a writer and it was at the end of 2013/beginning of 2014 and my business hadn't taken off as I would have liked. I was contemplating whether to get a job when one morning whilst doing my morning devotional, I felt drawn to the scripture 2 Kings 4:1-7, the story of the widow and the oil. In this story, there was a widow who was about to lose everything and through the Prophet Elisha, God told her to use what she had in her house (which was oil).

She was able to collect enough oil to sell and pay off her debts, with enough money left for her and her boys to live off. That scripture helped me to see what I had in my hand, and that was my writing.

I started to make writing a major focus in my business, and as a result I saw my business grow from strength to strength.

Dedicated to Marrissa, Felicia, Misha,
Veronique and Niamh - my fabulous nieces.
Don't let anyone ever put limitations on you and
what you can achieve, and most importantly,
don't put limitations on yourselves.

QUIETLY VISIBLE:

Leading with Influence and Impact as an Introverted Woman

BY CAROL STEWART

Published by
Filament Publishing Ltd
16, Croydon Road, Waddon, Croydon,
Surrey, CR0 4PA, United Kingdom
Telephone +44 (0)20 8688 2598
Fax +44 (0)20 7183 7186
info@filamentpublishing.com
www.filamentpublishing.com

ISBN 978-1-913192-69-3

Printed by IngramSpark

CONTENTS

FOREWORD

Removing the caps from your capacity is paramount for your personal and professional advancement. In *Quietly Visible*, Carol Stewart takes an academic and practical look at introverted women. She delves into deep issues around self-awareness, self-belief and desire, encouraging women to be intentional about increasing the capacity in the workplace.

Carol has created exercises that will help you to take a deeper, more forensic look at yourself, with a view to help you to erase the self-sabotaging thoughts that have the potential to dismantle purpose. Through business, work and life, we learn that in order to increase our capacity for more and to be able to fulfil the goals and purpose in life, there is a requirement for a physical ability to push on. This includes the ability to manage your personal energy more than managing time, because the expenditure of your energy is linked to time.

In addition to this, we must become proactive in dealing with emotions life teaches, and I've also come to know that thinking capacity is where the real progress is made. If you want to increase your overall success and lead effectively as an introverted woman, there is a requirement to increase your overall thinking capacity.

My coach John Maxwell taught me that when we upgrade our thoughts, it's a little bit like ice cubes versus icebergs. The difference between average thinkers and good thinkers is like the difference between ice cubes and icebergs; ice cubes are small and short-lived, whereas icebergs are huge and there is much more to them than meets the eye.

My suggestion to you today is to do those things that maximise your capacity. Carol speaks about this attitude, and she shares numerous real-life examples. In addition, she challenges you to make progress without losing the essence of your authentic self.

My desire for every woman that reads this book is that her character, discipline and attitude will grow taller and wiser in abundance so that she can live a life with no limits.

Claudine Reid MBE
Business Psychologist and Social Entrepreneur

INTRODUCTION

As a child I lacked confidence. In fact, my earliest memory of lacking confidence was just before I started school. I remember going along to visit the school with my mum and being in the school hall with all the other new starters and the teachers. All the other kids were happily playing with each other, but I was clinging to my mum. I was too scared to join in.

A lack of confidence was the story of my childhood, my teens and early 20s. At the age of 27, when my son was 6 years old, I became a single mum and I recognised that if I wanted him to grow up to be bold and confident, I needed to model that behaviour. As a result, I started to work on my self-development. I read books, had lots of training, coaching and so on, and I began to realise that I was doing things that a lot of my 'confident', more outgoing friends didn't have the confidence to do. I came to realise that it wasn't that I lacked confidence, it's that I was quiet. I was quiet but confident. Once I accepted myself as being quiet and that it was ok, I saw my confidence levels soar.

At that time, I didn't know much about introversion and extroversion, but I would often think to myself that I was different to a lot of my colleagues. I would go to area leadership meetings and many of my colleagues would be quite vocal, getting a lot of attention, whereas I would often remain quiet, only speaking when I had something of value to say. My manager would often tell me I should speak up more at meetings and tell everyone about the wonderful things that I was doing. But that wasn't me. It felt uncomfortable. Besides, I preferred to let my results speak for themselves and showcase my successes without making it me, me, me.

Because of my mistaken perception of what introversion was, I still hadn't made the connection that I was actually an introvert. It wasn't until I did the Myers Briggs test (see page 17 for explanation) at work that it hit me in the face. I was an introvert. The whole area leadership team did the test as a group at one of our meetings. As I uncovered my results, I was filled with disappointment. My results were ISTJ (introverted, sensing, thinking and judging) which, as described by Myers Briggs, means *'Quiet, serious, earn success by thoroughness and dependability. Practical, matter-of-fact, realistic, and responsible. Decide logically what should be done and work toward it steadily, regardless of distractions. Take pleasure in making everything orderly and organised – their work, their home, their life. Value traditions and loyalty.'*[1] I checked and double checked my score to make sure that I had added it up correctly, hoping that I had made a mistake. I didn't want to identify as introverted because there were so many negative connotations associated with the word. Shy. Lacking confidence. Boring. Socially recluse. Socially awkward. These were just some of the words that came to mind. Even the word introvert sounded limiting to me back then.

The word extrovert, on the other hand, sounded more positive, upbeat and outgoing, fitting the expectations of what society and the workplace here in the UK considered to be the best. I felt embarrassed having to stand up and openly say what my score was. I saw it as a negative. When we did an exercise where we had to stand in a corner of the room based on our ratings, I cringed, being one of the few introverts in the room. The extroverts were always the ones who were popular and got all the attention. That was something that I had become accustomed to all my life.

Even though I was quiet, I liked certain social environments which, in my limited understanding, introverts weren't supposed to enjoy. Whilst you wouldn't see me dancing on the table, I liked to party with the best of them. I wasn't, however, a social butterfly who worked the room. I would be quite happy to stand in a corner and listen and observe.

In 2011 when I left employment to start my coaching business and complete an MSc Coaching Psychology, that is when I got to know and accept myself as the introverted woman that I was. That and having found God and becoming a Christian two years earlier gave me a new level of confidence. Studying personality types, particularly the work of Carl Jung, helped me to realise exactly what it meant to be an introvert. But not only that, the more I studied it and reflected on who I was and what introversion meant, the more I began to realise that it was perfectly ok to be introverted – so I became introvert and proud. I now understood why I was the way I was. With that understanding, acceptance, and continued self-development, I was able to identify how to thrive in environments that are geared towards extroverted personalities.

A few years after starting my business, I had an 'aha' moment. I was reflecting on the clients that I had worked with, and one thing many of them had in common was that they too were introverted. All were doing well in their careers, but were mainly working in extroverted environments. Many of them felt they had to behave like the extroverts to be heard, taken seriously and to get on. This put a lot of pressure on them, and whilst all appeared good on the outside, and they were doing well in their work, on the inside it was a different matter. For many of them, there was an internal conflict going on between the persona they were adopting in their corporate roles as leaders, and who they really were on the inside.

There is only so long we can try to be something that we are not before it starts taking its toll on us. Putting pressure on ourselves in this way can be stressful. As that stress builds up, it can affect the way we start to see ourselves and it can seep into other areas of our lives. When we are stressed, we are more likely to have irrational thoughts about ourselves, and that in turn can affect our confidence and our ability to perform at our best.

I started writing articles about introversion and the challenges introverted women face in the corporate world, and the floodgates opened. I became inundated with messages and emails from women (and men) from all over the world who had been made to feel like they were second-rate citizens because they were introverted. In some of the stories, it was unbelievable that in this day and age, people were being treated this way. One woman told me that she went for an interview where the interviewer said that her biggest reservation about possibly hiring her was that she was introverted. She was asked to defend why she should be given a chance in the role. She said it made her wonder whether some extroverts really do see introversion as a disadvantage in the workplace.

My articles were republished on CNBC (the American Business news channel), The Muse and other platforms, and I was invited to be interviewed on podcasts. I then went on to be named a LinkedIn Top Voice UK 2017, 2018 and 2019. My initial plan wasn't to write a book about introversion. I planned to write a book about women leaving the corporate world and starting their own businesses, and the mindset challenges they face. I had even interviewed 12 successful business women, transcribed their interviews and started writing that book. However, because of the response I got to my articles about introversion, and feeling pained by the challenges introverted women across the world were experiencing, I felt compelled to write this book instead. I want to help these women fall in love with their introverted selves and to be introvert and proud.

Because of the unfavourable bias that exists towards introverts, I decided to make introversion my area of specialism. Couple that with the unfavourable bias that exists towards women in senior leadership roles, I decided to make supporting introverted women who are senior leaders my area of focus, which evolved into me becoming known as The Coach for High Achieving Introverted Women. Now I help quiet women to be great leaders and to lead with influence and impact. Whilst I work with both introverts and extroverts, because corporate culture is very much geared towards extroversion, I decided to make it my mission to change the narrative. I decided to raise awareness of the unfavourable bias that exists towards introversion and to help introverted women to accept themselves as they are (even if they don't realise they are not doing this), and to thrive in their careers and businesses whilst being their true, authentic, introverted selves.

This book does not subscribe to one particular theory on personality and is not based on the underpinnings of a personality test e.g. Big Five, Myers Briggs, 16PF etc. It is for those women who identify as being introverted, regardless of whether or not they have taken a personality test.

It is written from my experience as an introverted black woman, the daughter of immigrants from the Windrush Generation, and someone who was low in confidence and self-belief due to a lack of understanding of who I was, who has grown to accept and love myself as I am. It is from my experience as someone who felt that they didn't always fit in, yet progressed from one of the most junior roles in an organisation to that of senior leader. As well as my research, this book also draws on the lived experience of introverted women that I have coached and worked with. I have also sifted through over 1,200 responses to my articles on introversion and drawn from conversations with the 3,600+ women from my online communities, particularly the 600+ introverted women in my groups specifically for introverted women. These women have shared their stories with me and completed my surveys.

When many of my clients come to me for coaching, they present a particular issue, e.g. wanting a promotion, to change careers, increase their leadership effectiveness and so on, however, most often there is an underlying issue that is holding them back. Self-limiting beliefs and/or a lack of self-acceptance are often the internal barriers to them achieving their career and leadership goals. Before they address the presenting issue, we work on the underlying issues. Otherwise it would be difficult for them to confidently move forward in the way that they want to.

This book is a guide for you if you are an introverted woman who wants to be visible in what you do, and wants to lead with influence and impact, without having to change who you are. If you are someone who leads or coaches introverted women, it will give you an insight into the challenges they face and how you can support them to overcome those challenges. It will also help to increase your awareness of the unfavourable bias that exists towards introverts in the workplace. Whilst each chapter is stand-alone, and can be read in any order you choose, it is written in the order that works best when coaching my clients.

I take you through the process of accepting yourself as being introverted and being your authentic self. Then I help you to address the self-limiting beliefs of self-doubt, imposter syndrome and perfectionism before moving on to helping you with the common areas that introverted women find challenging in their careers. I show you how to thrive in an extroverted environment, and how you can position and promote yourself as a leader. I finish with how you can be an influential and impactful leader.

Although I have identified common themes and patterns, this is only a sample of introverted women worldwide. Everyone is different and deals with their situations differently. I present you with what the research shows, what my clients' experiences have been, my own personal experience, and that of the women worldwide who have told me their stories. Names have been changed for confidentiality reasons.

As you read the book, completing the exercises and self-reflection questions will help to increase your self-awareness, and in doing so, make it easier for you to see what you can do differently in order to become the best you. I suggest you keep a journal as you read, to capture the thoughts, reflections and 'aha' moments you have along the way.

1 | *Why a Book for Introverted Women Leaders?*

Maybe it was the bright orange top. Or maybe it was the fact that it was a noisy, social, networking event and I wasn't cowering away in a corner. Whatever it was, once when networking I was told by a woman that I didn't look like an introvert. It got me wondering what on earth an introvert is supposed to look like. On social media, I asked the question, 'When you think of an introvert, what words come to mind?' I got such responses as socially awkward, shy, nervous, lacking confidence, social misfit, anti-social, misunderstood, social anxiety, and more. I then turned to my trusted friend Google, and got more of the same.

There are many misconceptions about introverts, which arise from a lack of understanding as to what introversion is and what it isn't. The responses I got to my question on social media were misconceptions. Some of these things could apply to people who identify as being extroverted as well. These misconceptions have come about because the society we live in has become accustomed to larger-than-life personalities being the ones that get heard, and in doing so, get on. Where does this come from? Is it all about power and the fight for survival? We see this in all walks of life. Look at the school playground, for example. The popular, outgoing children are the ones who have other children latching on to hang out with them: children who want to be accepted, who want to belong to the group and don't want to be ostracised. If they are, they will feel cast out and rejected.

For introverted women leaders who have not yet seen the light (and by seen the light I mean have not yet recognised that introversion is something to be celebrated not ashamed of), working in environments that are dominated by extroverts can lead them to believe that there is something wrong with them. With a reported 98% of senior executive positions held by extroverts[1] and only 9.8% of executive directors of FTSE 100 companies being women[2], these facts can be discouraging for the introverted woman who is a leader and wants to get ahead in her career.

Historically, a leader in the UK has been associated with being a white, extroverted, alpha male. Introverted women are hit with a double whammy when it comes to leadership progression, being a woman and being introverted. And if they fall into any other underrepresented group such as BAME, disability, LGBT, age, etc that are more likely to be treated unfavourably, intersectionality[3] is at play. They can then fall even lower in the pecking order when it comes to getting the recognition and reward that they deserve.

With the knowledge and understanding of who they are, how they can utilise their introverted strengths, and why the barriers towards introverts exist in the corporate world, introverted women will be better equipped to break down those barriers. Either that, or they can choose which battles are worth taking on and which ones they need to let go of and move on from.

Here are five common misconceptions about introversion that I regularly encounter:

1. ALL INTROVERTS ARE SHY

Despite the first listing on Google defining introvert as meaning shy and reticent, not all introverts are shy.

Someone who is shy is said to be nervous or timid in the company of other people and someone who is reticent is said to not reveal their thoughts and feelings readily. Both could equally apply to extroverts. Some introverts are very confident when they are in the company of other people, just as some extroverts are not.

2. ALL INTROVERTS LACK CONFIDENCE

Because someone is an introvert, it doesn't automatically mean that they lack confidence. Likewise, because someone is an extrovert, it doesn't automatically mean that they are oozing with confidence.

As an introvert, I am a confident person and I know many other introverts who are confident too. Confidence doesn't mean you must be loud and talking all the time. To me, confidence means being comfortable with who I am and having the courage to do all that I need to do. From my experience, sometimes the way an extrovert's lack of confidence shows up is that they go into overdrive with the talking, and talk non-stop. For some introverts, a lack of confidence causes them to withdraw into themselves.

3. INTROVERTS HATE PUBLIC SPEAKING

I love public speaking. I can become quite animated when I am speaking on a topic that I am passionate about. It's the same for many other introverts. Get us on that stage and we will certainly give you a great, engaging performance. Yes, there are some introverts that hate public speaking but, you know what, there are extroverts who hate it too.

I often find that those who hate public speaking (both introverts and extroverts) dislike it because deep down they fear rejection, or that they will fail at it. They believe that they won't be any good at it, or that people won't like what they have to say. Some think that they will get asked a question that they can't answer, or that they will make a complete fool of themselves.

I have noticed an increasing assumption that public speaking means you have to do it in a loud, run on to the stage, high-fiving, Tony Robbins, turn to the person next to you style. This is totally opposite to how many introverts are. In fact, that style of public speaking makes many introverts cringe to watch (extroverts take note if you want to engage the introverts in the audience). When introverts do public speaking in our own authentic way, we too can light up the stage.

4. INTROVERTS DON'T LIKE NETWORKING

Some introverts like networking, whereas some introverts don't. Just as some extroverts like it and some of them hate it. For both introverts and extroverts, if they are shy and lacking confidence, they may not enjoy it.

In my experience, the reason why the introverts who are not shy and who don't lack confidence don't like networking is because they don't like making small talk. They don't like flitting around a room like a social butterfly speaking to as many people as they possibly can, the way some networking events are set up.

We prefer to have more deep and meaningful conversations with maybe one or two people. Some of us also don't like those noisy, large social environments, particularly if there is loud music on at the same time as you are trying to talk. Talking over the noise in such a buzzing environment can be draining and zap the energy out of us.

5. INTROVERTS DON'T OPEN UP ABOUT HOW THEY ARE FEELING

There are many introverts AND extroverts who don't open up about how they are feeling. Sometimes it's a trust issue. Sometimes it's because we are private people. Given the right conditions, we introverts have been known to bare our souls. To say all introverts don't open up and don't show how they are feeling is a bit like saying all men can't multitask.

Introvert or extrovert, we are all created equal. It's just that in a quest for power, some of us have marginalised others along the way, and in the case of introverts and extroverts in the corporate world, it is often those who shout loudest who get heard. This is sometimes even when it is not the best or the right thing to do.

There are plenty of resources available that can give you an in-depth insight into introversion and extroversion, so I don't go into detail here. I do however give a brief overview so you can see how some of the thinking around it has developed over the years, for those of you who have little knowledge of the concept. Carl Jung was the founder of analytical psychology and popularised the term introversion/extroversion in the 1920s. He categorised the way human beings act and react into two attitude types namely extroverts (the original spelling was extravert from the Latin meaning of extra, i.e. outwards, and *vertere* meaning 'to turn'. In this book I use the popular, modern spelling extrovert) and introverts. Extroverts are more able to deal with things that are external to the mind and introverts are more able to deal with the interior personalities of their mind[4].

To cut a long story short, he also categorised people into the following four function types according to their preference of gathering information and making decisions:

- Sensation – likes things to be specific
- Intuition – acting on hunches
- Thinking – what is fair and true
- Feeling – what it is worth for us

Sensation and Intuition are concerned with gathering information and are (as he termed) irrational functions. Thinking and Feeling are concerned with making decisions and are rational functions.

The way in which we perceive information will determine our preference. People who are exposed to natural conditions use their intuition a lot, as do people who take risks in unknown fields. Intuition is a perception that goes by the unconscious. Each person has one of the four dominant functions.

Combining the two attitude types and the four functional types provides eight psychological types. These psychological types have been further developed to form many psychologically-based personality tests (which you may be familiar with) such as Myers and Briggs who added judging and perception to create the 16 psychological types we know today, in the Myers Briggs test, known as MBTI.

Jung's typology can be somewhat misguided as the traits introversion and extroversion sit on a continuum and people may fall into different points along the continuum. There may be certain factors that affect where an individual sits on the continuum, according to the environment and what is going on for them at that moment in time. For example, although I am an introvert, there are situations and environments where I veer towards the extroverted side of the continuum.

In the 1960s psychologist Hans J Eysenck found that introverts are more arousable and that our brains are more active (cortical arousal) from things that happen externally to us. That's why high-intensity social stimulations, such as loud parties, can make us over-aroused. At rest, extroverts' brains are low in activity. They experience less cortical arousal from a given stimulus, and they therefore seek out more intense social experiences.[5] Because being in high-intensive socially stimulating environments can make introverts over-aroused, we may avoid putting ourselves in such uncomfortable environments.

This knowledge in itself was quite revelatory to me. Knowing this, I am able to exercise self-care and put things in place to enable me to recharge when I have been in overly stimulating environments. When I was first starting my coaching business, I faced challenges getting going. I knew what I needed to do, but I just wasn't making the progress that I wanted. I came to realise that networking was an issue and that I was avoiding it. As someone new to business, networking was going to be pivotal for me in getting my name out there, raising my profile and ultimately getting clients. Prior to my gaining an understanding of introversion and extroversion, I thought I lacked confidence in networking. Although I discuss this in more detail in the chapter on networking, I came to realise that it was the cortical arousal that caused me discomfort. Over the years I have grown to love networking; however, there are certain networking environments that I will avoid where possible.

Eysenck suggested that there is a biological basis as to whether someone is an introvert or extrovert and is well known for his lemon drop test. He asked participants to taste a few drops of lemon juice, and found that introverts salivated in response to the juice more than those whom he identified as extroverts. He believed that the role of the Reticular Activating System (RAS) area of the brain could extend to areas such as taste and social interaction. In introverts, the increased activation of RAS might explain the increased saliva on the taste of lemon juice. It might also support Eysenck's belief that this internal activation provides introverts with a sufficient level of stimulation, leading them to sometimes become overwhelmed in demanding social situations and preferring to be on their own or in the company of smaller, quieter groups[6].

Eysenck identified that introversion/extroversion is partly hereditary and partly influenced by childhood experiences. Extroverted and introverted tendencies appear earlier in adulthood and evidence more stability through the developmental years than most personality characteristics[7]. Both my parents are introverts, as are my siblings, however my son is very much an extrovert. In fact, he could be quite a drain on my energy when he was a child. Always wanting stimulation, everything had to be made into a game with him.

If we were sitting waiting in the GP surgery, he would want to play 'shin chan wala' (when I was a child I knew it as 'paper, scissors, stone') or 'I spy'. If we were travelling on the London Underground, the game would be to guess which side the doors were going to open on, the winner being the one with the most correct answers by the end of the journey. Walking to school, it was a game of who could be the first to spell a word from the letters on the car registration plates that we passed. Again, the winner was the one who got the most words. As an introverted single mum who worked full time, first thing in the morning when I wanted a bit of solitude as I embraced the school run and navigated my way to a busy day ahead, playing overly stimulating games was not my preference...

Since Carl Jung, we have also seen the emergence of the Big Five factor model of personality, for which extroversion is one of five types, and others. More recently, we have seen the Four Factor S.T.A.R. model[8], which categorises introversion into four areas (S.T.A.R. being an acronym), namely:

Social – Social preference is in depth of personal relationships over breadth, and in quieter social activities rather than overstimulating social environments.

Thinking – Based upon cognitive introspectiveness. Includes all aspects of thought, matters of deliberation, reflection, and emotional significance attached to an object or event.

Anxious – Concerned how viewed by others. A lack of understanding of others. Socially withdrawn. Tendency to ruminate.

Restrained – Reserved. Inhibited. Avoids overstimulation. Preference to think before speaking, rather than acting in the moment. Decision making may take longer due to a preference for longer processing of information.

Even before modern-day psychologists were looking at this, the ancient philosophers had voiced their perspectives on it, and certain cultures embrace introversion as a leadership quality. Nordic countries and countries such as Japan and China in particular are well known for their introverted cultures.

Extroverts are typically known as being more outgoing, bold, assertive and cheerful than introverts, and in our individualistic Western culture, it would appear from the evidence that extroverts fit in better and thrive better than introverts[9]. Because of the individualism of our Western society, people tend to place more emphasis on personal attainment as opposed to the collective attainment. As a result, we see more of a need for greater self-esteem, and the quest for personal happiness. Seeking this self-validation can appear as overconfidence, something more attributed to extroverts[10]. Many people sit somewhere in the middle and have both introverted and extroverted traits and are known by the term 'ambivert'.

Embracing our differences helps to make organisations dynamic. Whilst a lot is talked about the most obvious differences that are seen, and to some extent differences that aren't seen such as religion, sexual preference and so on, one difference that often gets overlooked and unspoken about is personality.

When looking at diversity and inclusion, personality should be part of the mix as well. Personality Homophily, where we have a tendency to associate with people who have a similar personality to us, is often at play in organisations. In the workplace, this can translate to an unconscious bias towards different personality types. Where a personality doesn't fit the dominant cultural norm, it could lead to the individual being treated less favourably.

I frequently get messages or emails from introverted women working in organisations with a predominately extroverted culture, who feel the pressure of working in an environment that doesn't accept their difference. It has been said that the more homogeneous an organisation is, the greater the likelihood of a tendency to be drawn to people like themselves. If there is a homogeneous personality in an organisation, where does this leave those whose personality doesn't fit the majority? We also see this with cliques; how often have you seen cliques form in the workplace, of people who are very similar to each other?

Research suggests that to a certain degree, organisations are homogeneous when it comes to the personality traits of their managers[11]. This becomes more so the higher up the corporate ladder you go. This leads to a lack of diversity and inclusion regarding personality types. For those aspiring to leadership roles, seeing a dominant personality type in leadership teams that is unlike them is hardly going to give them encouragement to progress in the organisation. A key factor influencing an individual's decision to join an organisation is a personality fit, but often it's not until they are actually in the organisation that they realise that it isn't a fit.

Some of the benefits to be gained from having diverse personalities in the workplace include:

- Better quality decisions
- Better teamwork
- Creativity and innovation
- Challenging of assumptions

I regularly coach introverted leaders for whom there is not a personality fit between them and the homogeneous extroverted personalities on the leadership team. Many are weary from trying to make it fit. The support they get through coaching enables them to be their authentic self and thrive in those environments, and there are some who opt to find an organisation for which there is a better fit.

When it comes to hiring or promoting, a lot of organisations look for a cultural fit. The danger with this is that unfavourable unconscious bias towards different personalities can creep in. I recently had a conversation with a woman who was unsuccessful at an interview because she wasn't a cultural fit. She wasn't given any specifics as to what this meant so was left to draw her own meaning.

Having individuals that are a cultural fit can be good for both the individual and the organisation. The individual is more likely to have greater job satisfaction, is more likely to be committed, and is more likely to stay at the organisation. And whilst organisations may want their employees to share the same values and norms, hiring for cultural fit can lead to discriminatory practices if not handled properly.

Many recruiting decisions are done on the basis of personality tests, but could these unwittingly lead to unfair treatment towards different personality types? Whilst such tests may provide valuable data for some organisations, there is also the possibility that they could lead to unfavourable treatment, or at its worst, discrimination. In 2017, an employment appeals tribunal (EAT) held that the use of a psychometric test was discriminatory[12]. The EAT held that an applicant for a solicitors' training scheme who has Asperger's syndrome suffered unlawful disability discrimination when she was required to sit a test in a multiple-choice format in the recruitment process. Whilst this case involved a claim for disability discrimination, it highlights the potential for the results of such tests to be discriminatory in their use. Personality tests should not be used in isolation in selection processes, as having too many people with the same trait leads to a lack of diversity.

Unfavourable bias towards introverts is not only present in the recruitment process, but other HR processes are potentially unfavourably biased as well. In 2017 I was approached by Sarah Burdakay, HR Director and Coach, who had recently discovered that she was an ambivert, and who wanted to counteract the extrovert bias that seems to occur in so many HR processes

such as assessment centres and learning styl
invited me to co-author an article with her for ⅈ⍳ⅉ .
Director magazine. Our article, *The Shy, The Brash and
The Talkative*, was published in the December 2017
issue[13]. The article illustrates why talent management
strategies may unwittingly be putting many people at a
disadvantage and challenges HR Directors to examine
whether their organisation is unconsciously biased
against their introverted employees.

Leaders should regularly challenge their views and
assumptions and get feedback from others by seeking
different perspectives, so they are not closed minded. In
turn, they should challenge the views and assumptions
of others who demonstrate personality bias. If you are a
leader, develop an awareness of how you interact with
different personality types. Having that awareness will
enable you to recognise when you are treating someone
less favourably because their personality is different. If
you don't interact well with those who have different
personalities, spend more time with them and develop
ways in which you can. Examine the decisions you have
made about other people, looking at your reasons
for making those decisions and what aspect their
personality played in your decision-making process.

There is more to personality than introversion and
extroversion and whilst I don't like to limit people by
putting a label on them, sometimes labels are necessary.
Not to keep us in boxes, but to enable us to identify
why we may be the way we are and gain a deeper
understanding of this. By having a name that described

why I was the way that I was, once I understood introversion, I was able to embrace it and see how this was in actual fact a strength. I do not mind using the word introverted when describing aspects of myself. Additionally, labels are sometimes necessary in order to call out bias, and to change the narrative and the negative connotations associated with certain words.

Like many other high-achieving introverted women, I used to see introversion as a weakness, focusing on the fact that I didn't match up to the gregarious extroverts around me. Because of society's favourable bias towards extroverts, this can cause introverts to doubt themselves, believing that something is wrong with them. For example, not being able to shoot from the hip, rather than having a preference to think, reflect and then give a carefully considered response. When networking, not being able to work the room, making small talk and speaking to as many people as possible, rather than having deep and meaningful conversations with a few people and really being able to connect with them.

Some women are unaccepting of their introversion and put on a false persona, trying to be something that they are not, in order to be accepted and fit in. Prior to receiving coaching, each day Sally would turn up for work in her role as Deputy Vice-President and she would put on her mask. Her mask was this pretentious, high-energy, laugh-out-loud persona that her colleagues saw each day. To the outside world she was confident, sassy and gave as good as she got. But on the inside, it felt as if she was in turmoil. It felt to her as if she was trapped and suffocating. Stuck on a treadmill and unable to get off, she knew that if she continued like this, she would burn out from the stress and exhaustion of it all.

I come across many 'Sallys' in my work. They act this way because of the unfavourable bias shown towards them as introverts and because of having to contend with the systems and environments that exist within the corporate structure that are geared towards extroverted personalities. This book is needed for these women, to show them that they can peel off the mask, they don't need to pretend, and that they can show up as themselves AND still be great leaders.

When women request to join my High Achieving Introverted Women Facebook group (which is for introverted women who are leaders or aspiring leaders), one of the questions they have to answer before being accepted into the group is what challenges they experience because they are introverted. Invariably the same responses come up time and time again. It may be written in a different way, but nevertheless, they boil down to the same issues. These are speaking up and being heard, feeling drained, doubting themselves, struggling with networking, being misunderstood and so on.

Whether it is the open plan office, the endless meetings, or simply that the louder personalities are the ones that get heard, these challenges affect women all over the world. Whether you are in your 20s or your 50s, whether you are in a very senior role or in the most junior role, without the awareness that this book will raise for you, you will continue to not be your best possible self.

As an introverted woman, being in denial and unaccepting of your difference to your extroverted colleagues can be like trying to fit a square peg into a round hole. This can negatively impact your self-confidence and self-belief, impacting on your performance and ability to thrive as a leader.

Over recent years, we have seen a move to more large, open plan offices which can be an introvert's nightmare. An overemphasis on group work rather than solitude time can be draining for the introverted woman. Activities such as brainstorming, and the way meetings are set up, don't allow for the thinking and reflecting time that introverts typically prefer. Just a few tweaks to these corporate activities can make them more inclusive to all. Something as simple as sending out the agenda and papers for meetings in sufficient time can make a big difference.

There needs to be a shift in the way introversion is perceived. The stereotypes need to be broken. The negative label that was attached and that has stuck over the years needs to be torn down. It is said that the negative association towards introversion came about from psychoanalyst Sigmund Freud. When Carl Jung first presented his thoughts on introversion, he viewed it as being normal: a polar opposite on the continuum to extroversion.[14] He recognised that people can operate on different ends of the continuum, dependent on the environment and their circumstances.

Jung believed it was an error to force a child in the opposite direction to what they were[15], but we still see children and adults made to feel like something is wrong with them and made to feel like they need to be different because of their introverted nature. Someone recently told me about their introverted daughter being very upset because she had been marked down a grade in her school work. The reason the teacher gave was that she didn't put her hand up enough in class. Many of the women I coach had similar experiences when they were children that have affected their self-belief as adults.

In environments that I am familiar with, with people that I know well and that I am close to, I can at times be the life and soul of the party. Jung saw introversion as being a natural phenomenon, whereas Freud made it seem as if it was something introverts needed to recover from. Over the years this has stuck. As Western society has become more concerned with the self, it's as if there has become a greater emphasis on the energetic personality as being the 'best'.

Before coming to me for coaching, Caroline was very talkative when amongst family and close friends, finding it easy to speak up and speak out when she was with them. Yet at work, she found speaking up very challenging. She would keep quiet at meetings, rather than expressing her point of view. She would have something on her mind but not speak up about it, only to find one of her colleagues voice the very thing that she'd had on her mind. She would then feel bad about herself afterwards for not speaking up, and condemn herself for it. Or take Belinda, who felt confident speaking in front of hundreds of people at the annual conference of the charity of which she was Chair of in a voluntary capacity, but yet in meetings with the rest of the leadership team in her corporate role, found it difficult to speak up. I cover this in more detail in Chapter 3 where we will look at the common internal challenges that affect introverted women and hold them back.

Research shows that introverts are less likely to emerge as leaders, but there is little research as to why this is. It could be because introverts are less likely to take the lead amongst teams because they perceive that putting on the extroverted behaviour that will be required of them will have a negative effect on them[16]. I hope this book will help you to develop strategies that enable you to view more positively those situations where a more extroverted type of behaviour is required, and also to get the best outcome you want from them. Just because something causes you to lose energy, it doesn't automatically mean that you are a bad fit for it[17].

When we look at celebrities, speakers and leaders who are extroverted, they are the ones that seem to get the most attention (and maybe it's because they are more likely to put themselves in the limelight), but not everyone warms to that type of personality. A comment on one of my articles once said that the phrase introverted leaders was an oxymoron. The person was saying that introverts could not be leaders because the term itself was contradictory, meaning two totally opposite things. This in itself is a misconception.

We have (and have had) some great introverted leaders. Mark Zuckerberg, Bill Gates, Barack Obama, Rosa Parks, Eleanor Roosevelt and Oprah Winfrey, are just a few who are reported to be introverts. There is, however, little reported on introverted women in the corporate space, and if there is, they are not always portrayed in a positive light. For example, putting politics aside, former Prime Minister Theresa May was often given a hard time by the press, earning the nickname 'Maybot'.

There are a growing number of books for introverts already written, so why do we need another book is a question I asked myself. But nobody has lived my experience, or worked with my clients in the way that I have and learnt from that experience, or engaged with the many, many introverted women through my articles and online communities in the way that I have was my response.

Despite the likes of books such as *Quiet: The Power of Introverts in a World that Can't Stop Talking* by Susan Cain, and *The Introvert Advantage* by Dr Marti Olsen Laney some 10 years prior to that, introverts are still very much given a raw deal in the corporate environment. Things are thankfully (albeit slowly) changing, though, and I hope that this book adds to the growing body of written work that is raising awareness and bringing about change, and helps to change the narrative introverted women have about themselves.

CHAPTER

2 | *Being Yourself*

For women climbing the corporate ladder, we are all familiar with the challenges that this poses the more senior that you get. And if introverts only account for 2% of senior executives[1], despite making up to 50% of the population, where does this leave the introverted woman who is a leader? For many, it's putting on a mask and suppressing their authentic voice as they try to put on a persona that makes them feel accepted and get taken seriously as leaders in the extroverted environments that they work in. But what do you think that this does over time?

Over time, it puts pressure on you and can cause emotional distress. It can chip away at your self-confidence and self-belief, and drain your energy. This has been the case for many of the introverted women I have coached who have tried to act extroverted over a period of time. That is why if you are to be a confident, influential and impactful leader, it is best to be your authentic self, whilst adapting to different situations and environments. For many years personality psychologists have reported that extroverts are happier more of the time than introverts.[2] Could this be one of the contributing factors as to why extroversion appears to be more highly favoured in the workplace, and why people are encouraged to act more extroverted? In her book *Quiet: The Power of Introverts in a World that Can't Stop Talking*, Susan Cain refers to the 'extrovert ideal'. She describes it as an omnipresent belief that the ideal self is gregarious, alpha and comfortable in the spotlight.

> 'Introverts living under the Extrovert Ideal are like women in a man's world, discounted because of a trait that goes to the core of who they are.' Susan Cain[3]

This is something I can certainly relate to, as can my clients. As mentioned previously, when I did the Myers Briggs test, I was unhappy with my result for this very reason. It is why, I believe, many introverted women think that they have to act extroverted if they are to get ahead as leaders. We see it in all spheres of life here in the UK, from schools, to workplaces, to churches – particularly the Pentecostal churches, of which I am a member of one.

I think former Prime Minister Theresa May gave us some great examples of inauthenticity. Observing her over the years, it was clear that she was introverted. Her exit speech has been reported as the most passionate one she made and one in which I believe she was being her authentic self. The times when she tried to appear more personable, she came over stiff and inauthentic. Running onto the stage to the sounds of Abba's Dancing Queen at the party conference à la Tony Robbins had many people cringing in their seats. She looked fake and uncomfortable as she tried to be something she's not.

Getting to a place where you confidently show up as your authentic, introverted self is freeing. There's no mask, no pretence, just you being you. I would add a word of caution, though, when it comes to being your authentic self. Whilst being your true self means you don't have to put on a persona that is so uncomfortable it's obvious to other people you are acting disingenuously, you will need to challenge yourself to step out of your comfort zone and stretch yourself in potentially uncomfortable ways, if you are to be the impactful leader you want to be. For example, as a leader you may need to respond to people and situations that require you to act in ways that don't play to your introverted strengths, such as needing to make an on-the-spot decision, whereas your preferred, natural way of being is to think and reflect first. I cover how you can adapt in such situations in a later chapter, but for now, it is essential that you are aware that sticking too long with comfortable behaviour can prevent you from adapting to new and different situations.[4]

Likewise, being your authentic self doesn't mean you have a licence to chill. If you are to be influential and impactful as a leader, you need to be aware of how your behaviour impacts others. You also need to have an awareness of how to get the best out of the people you lead, not to mention stakeholders, clients/customers and those more senior than you as well, which at times, requires you to adapt your behaviour. If you are so quiet and reserved that you come across as an ice maiden, that is not going to help people to warm to you or help you to exercise influence. Be your authentic self, but develop a growth mindset and your emotional intelligence. Having a growth mindset will enable you to still adapt to situations, without compromising who you are.

A lack of understanding of what introversion is can lead you to believe that you lack confidence or that you're not good enough because you don't fit the 'extrovert ideal'. I mentioned previously that I lacked confidence and had a belief that I was not good enough to be part of the popular crowd. Add to that, I was the only black girl amongst my classmates, so being different in this way fed my insecurities and a lack of acceptance of who I truly was.

Even when I accepted myself as I was, I still was not expressing my authentic voice. I didn't see the point of speaking just for speaking's sake. I would contribute at meetings if I had something of value to add, not just to add noise, and most definitely not to boast about my achievements. In his book Introverts in the Church, Adam McHugh mentions how extroverts talk in order to think and introverts think in order to talk[5], which is something that I can very much relate to.

Running my own business means that I am often in situations that are not conducive to me thriving as an introvert. Self-awareness, self-belief, and a desire for continuous learning and development enables me to put myself into those situations, and still be my best self, or strive to be my best by developing and growing. I recognised how my introverted strengths had played out over the years in my leadership career. Remaining calm in a crisis, being reflective, not throwing my toys out of the pram, making carefully considered decisions rather than shooting from the hip, giving others the freedom to use their own initiative, having good listening skills and more.

I was sitting in my office one lunchtime and overheard a conversation in which a couple of people were talking about someone, referring to them as a Rottweiler. They weren't aware that I was in earshot and could hear what they were saying so I thought I'd better make them know I could hear them before they said anything further. They told me that they weren't talking about me because I most certainly wasn't a Rottweiler; I was more like a Poodle. This was inference to my calm, quiet temperament as opposed to the louder and more extroverted, bullish temperament of my colleague.

I found that the more I utilised my strengths, rather than focusing on what I was not, the more confident I became in speaking up just as I am, acting in alignment to my values.

Authenticity is often described as the experience and expression of one's true self, and not being swayed by sociocultural influences that don't align with your values and beliefs.

Historically, the true self was described as being part of what was needed for an individual to live a fulfilling life.

Evidence suggests that here in the West, there may be an affiliation between those with a propensity for introversion and higher inauthenticity. However, I suspect that this is because of the extrovert ideal and an unspoken (and sometimes spoken) expectation to act more extroverted. One study found that those who were comfortable with being introverted showed higher levels of authenticity and well-being than those who wanted to be extroverted[6]. There was a time some years ago when I didn't have the confidence to be my authentic self. Over the years as I have accepted myself as I am, I have become more confident at expressing my authentic voice. If you are an introverted woman who feels the pressure from trying to be something that you're not, or who yearns to be like your extroverted colleagues, I encourage you to find your real voice. Take off the mask and give yourself the freedom that comes with being your true, authentic self.

START WITH SELF-ACCEPTANCE

So how do you be your authentic self? It starts with self-acceptance. Learn to love and accept yourself for who you are. When we are our authentic selves, we are naturally more confident, look more attractive, feel more attractive, and are less likely to look to others for approval and to feel valued than when we are not. For some introverted women, self-acceptance is a challenge. If we don't accept ourselves for who we are, it can lead us to doubt ourselves and our ability. It can cause us to adopt values imposed on us by other people (in particular the values of our parents or carers, and those who influenced us when we were growing up), our environments and more. It can cause us to be fearful and lacking in confidence. It can result in us not being able to see our gifts, talents, skills and strengths, and as a result not utilise them, and it can hold us back.

Mine has been a long journey to total self-acceptance, but one where I believe I have finally arrived. As a child, I had to contend with being different to my peers. There was my introversion, being black, my afro hair, my family's socio-economic status compared to my middle-class white friends... all of which contributed to me not being accepting of myself, and wanting to be something different. A lot of how I felt was as a result of conditioning. My being conditioned to believe that introverts weren't as well liked as extroverts. That long silky, blonde hair and blue eyes were the epitome of beauty. That coming from a working class, immigrant background meant that you weren't clever enough, good enough or popular enough, and that you needed to know your place.

Even when I had accepted myself as being a quiet person, and that it was ok, I still had not totally accepted who I was. Yes, I was confident. Yes, I was pursuing progression in my leadership career. But I hadn't totally accepted who

I was, because I was still concerned with other people's perceptions of me. Which at times would cause me to doubt myself and to question whether I could do certain things. It would make me think that because of my circumstances, certain things would not be easy for me. This would cause imposter syndrome (which I cover in the next chapter) to rear its head. As I was going through this, I wasn't aware that all of this was the underlying factor for why I saw myself the way that I did, and for the limitations that I put on myself. I didn't realise that this was why I felt about myself the way that I did.

That is why I love the natural hair movement amongst black women. For so long we have been led to believe that our hair is not good enough. As a child, I wished that I had hair like my white friends. My sister, friend and I would put cardigans or towels on our heads and pretend that we had long hair that could shake like our white friends. We had been conditioned to believe that our natural, kinky, afro hair was not good enough. And that is why today, we see so many black women wearing long weaves, hair which looks totally false, because of what we have been conditioned to believe about ourselves.

Yes, some of us wear our hair that way because it is convenient. But there are some who don't realise that wearing their hair that way is because of a lack of love for who they really are. As for me, I now love my natural hair. I love the fact that it is thick and doesn't blow in the wind. I love the fact that it is so versatile and I can do so many things with it. Hair routines that I used to despise as a child such as the washing and plaiting of it, I see as all part of maintaining this beautiful creation that is my hair. I love this beautiful creation that is my natural hair, that is a part of the authentic me.

You may be wondering what my story about my hair has to do with introverted women and leadership. It is to help illustrate my belief that it's not until we can become who we truly are that we can become who we are really meant to be. My hair was a part of my journey to becoming my authentic self. For you it may be something else. Along with accepting yourself as the beautiful, introverted woman that you are, there may be other things about yourself that you need to learn to love before you can become your authentic self.

You may look at extroverted people and think that you're not as good as them and put yourself down in the process, but please remember – you are not the same as anyone else. A bit like apples and pears; both are fruit that are grown from a seed, and are similar in size and texture, but they are different. They look different and they taste different, but they are both delicious fruits. Some people prefer apples, some people prefer pears, some people like both equally, some people don't like either, and you know what? That is ok. And that is how it is with us. Some people will like you, some people will not and some will be neutral. And you know what? That too is ok! Different strokes for different folks.

We are all unique individuals with different skills, abilities, gifts and talents. We each have things that we are good at, things we are not good at and things we are neutral about. Recognising and accepting this will help you to accept that introversion doesn't define you – it is a part of who you are. The following exercise will help with this:

Exercise

Take a sheet of paper and divide it into 3 columns, with the headings 'Things I am Good at', 'Things I am Not Good at' and 'Things I am Neutral about'. Then list all the things that you can think of that fit in to each of the columns. Things that you are good at, or what other people tell you that you are good at. With the things that you are not good at, only list things for which there is evidence to show that you are not good at them. Don't just think of things that are work related, think about things in your personal life, or about any voluntary work you may do. You will probably find that you have things in each of the columns, or you may find that you only have things in two of the columns. You may even be surprised and find that you have more in the things you are good at than you initially thought.

Having done the exercise, what does it tell you about yourself?

I do this exercise with my clients and they are always surprised by the results. With most of them, their initial thoughts before doing the exercise are that there are more things that they are not good at than they are good at. Doing this exercise gives them a nice, pleasant surprise. Many of them have gone through their lives focusing on what they're not good at, and by doing so, have not felt good about themselves in the process. Having more of an overview in this way gives them a more balanced outlook about themselves, making it easier for them to accept themselves for who they are.

By nature, we are fallible and imperfect, and in the words of Professor Stephen Palmer and Christine Wilding, '*The secret to true self-acceptance is to stop seeing ourselves as a single entity. We are made up of hundreds of component parts – our skills, abilities, physique, sporting or artistic leanings, levels of competitiveness, intelligence, emotional maturity, personal qualities... and many more*[7].

You may have imperfections, you may have weaknesses – we all do. Recognise you have them and look at what you can do to improve on them if needed, but don't dismiss yourself or deem yourself unworthy because of them. If you were to ask other people to do this exercise (including your extroverted friends and colleagues), they would have similar results, i.e. things listed in each of the columns. They may have similar things to you but listed under different headings. After all, we are all different to each other, and that is ok.

Janet would get home at the end of the day feeling stressed. She worked in an environment where she was the only introvert amongst a leadership team of extroverts. She would often put on an act because she thought that she wouldn't otherwise be considered as good as her extroverted colleagues, or wouldn't be taken seriously. Acting in this way was starting to take its toll on her, not only causing her to feel stressed, but causing her to continuously doubt herself. She knew she couldn't carry on like that for much longer, or it would have a negative impact on her health. As a child she had been led to feel that she wasn't good enough because she was quiet. Doing the exercise was revelatory for her. Because of the 'stuff' that had been put on her over the years, she hadn't been able to accept herself as she really was. With this recognition came self-acceptance. After years of not liking who she was, she was able to accept that she was good enough as herself.

ALIGN WITH YOUR PERSONAL VALUES

The second step in being your authentic self is aligning yourself with your personal values. Our values go to the core of who we are and are those things that really matter to us and that, if not present in our lives, can leave us feeling demotivated, unfulfilled, and even depressed. They are like our moral compass: a principle or belief that is fundamental to who we are and what we think is of high importance to us. It is important that both the way we live our lives, and our work, align with our values, because if they don't, we are incongruent. When you are making decisions about changes in your career, business and life, it is important to consider your values and whether what you are going to do aligns with them. If you are feeling unfulfilled in what you do, or in your life generally, or you are demotivated or unhappy, or have an inner struggle between who you really are and who you portray yourself as, reflect on whether you are aligned with your values.

My client Suzy was unhappy and unfulfilled at work, and as a result was feeling stressed. On giving her a values exercise to complete, she had an 'aha' moment when she realised that the way she was expected to treat customers did not align with her values, and that was why she felt so dissatisfied at work. With this realisation, she was able to look at finding work that was more in alignment. Being aligned to our values helps us to feel fulfilled, content, satisfied, motivated and to have an overall sense of wellbeing. How aligned to your values are you? If you are not sure what your values are, think about a time when you have experienced a personal offence. A time when someone did something or said something to you that you felt went against the grain of who you are and what you stand for. As an example, I was once asked to do some work for someone that I had worked for previously. The thing was, when I had done the work, it had been through an agency. This time they wanted to bypass the agency, and whilst I had not been asked to sign a non-compete agreement, it didn't feel right that they were bypassing the agency and coming directly to me. Integrity is a core value of mine and I felt that approaching me in this way lacked integrity.

To get further clarification on your values, you may find it helpful to complete the Values Exercise in the Appendix at the back of the book. Being in alignment with your personal values helps you to feel more authentic and to be perceived as authentic[8]. With many of the introverted women that I coach, they find that there is misalignment between who they really are and how they feel they should portray themselves in the workplace. They come to recognise that they are not being their authentic selves and have been acting that way because they felt that they had to if they wanted to be heard or taken seriously.

YOUR STRENGTHS

Our character strengths have been said to be the vehicle that lets us live out our values. When we exercise our character strengths, it leads to gratification and authenticity. Embedding our character strengths in our daily living increases wellbeing and enhances our levels of flourishing. Research shows that people who use their character strengths are three times more likely to report having an excellent quality of life and six times more likely to be engaged at work. If you don't know what your character strengths are, you can take this free scientifically validated test courtesy of Values in Action and also find out more about character strengths and virtues (please note, I am not affiliated with it).[9]

Our natural strengths enable us to be our best selves. When we utilise them, we are naturally more confident, more motivated and more likely to be in flow. When we are in flow, that is when we are at our best, and when we achieve peak performance. Our strengths are those things we do that come most naturally to us. When we use our strengths, we are happier, engaged and more likely to achieve our goals.

A word of caution, though. Whilst I'm all in favour of adopting a strengths-based approach, overusing them or not utilising them in the right way can actually hinder us if we are not careful. For example, Tina, one of my clients, wanted a promotion to Director. She was very clear on what her strengths were and how she used them. She was recognised for great performance with a motivated, engaged, high-performing team. But she had been putting too much emphasis on using her strengths in her role at the wrong level. She had not been utilising them in ways that would position her for the promotion that she wanted.

In order to position herself, it meant her having to do things such as networking and being more social, promoting herself and increasing her visibility, attending meetings at a senior level and speaking up more, all of which, because of her introverted nature, she found to be draining. Coaching her to adopt some of the strategies I outline in this book, she started to use her strengths in ways that enabled her to position herself and demonstrate her ability to perform at that more senior level. She started to network, take on some of the responsibilities from her manager and attend meetings with more senior personnel and stakeholders. At these meetings she would speak up and put forward her ideas and suggestions. She identified how she could do all this in ways that felt authentic, as well as how to manage her energy levels so she didn't feel drained.

Using your strengths will help you to feel and be authentic. If there is something that you want to achieve, like Tina, look at utilising your strengths to help you achieve it. What are your strengths and in what way do you utilise them in your work? In her book *Ordinary Women Doing Extraordinary Things*, Claudia Crawley suggests asking yourself the following questions and carefully considering the answers in order to help identify your strengths[10]:

I.   When I am performing most effectively, what am I doing?
II.   In which situations do I really feel like me? What am I doing?
III. What do people appreciate me for?
IV.   What do I do, that comes really easily to me?
V.   What skills do I have?
VI.   What qualifications do I have?

Having reflected on your answers to the above questions, what strengths stand out for you? In what ways are you utilising them? If you are not utilising them, what can you do differently in order to do so?

Over the years, I have found that the more true I became to myself, the less I wanted to act in ways that were not me. I was once amongst a group of extroverted people that I didn't know very well at the end of a very socially charged networking event. It was late in the evening and I was ready to go home and recharge. There was one person who had driven to the venue who offered to drop some of us home. Because of my self-awareness, I knew that because I felt drained, I wanted to withdraw more. On the journey, they were all talking ten to the dozen whilst I sat quietly listening and observing how the different personalities showed up, joining in when I felt I had something to contribute as opposed to trying to talk just for the sake of it.

Whilst sitting there, I reflected on how the old me would have felt slightly anxious, putting pressure on myself to talk more, making things worse in the process because of the pressure I was putting on myself, and as a result probably speaking less. Now I felt comfortable and confident being seen as the quiet one amongst the group, yet still making a valuable contribution to the discussion. However, I knew that if the circumstances had warranted it, I would have made more of an effort to talk.

Mary, a Senior Director, felt like she had to be someone different at work. She observed Vice-Presidents who were extroverted and felt like she needed to be more like them. She also felt disingenuous, pretending to be interested in topics or discussions that she had no interest in. This caused an internal conflict for her, and she felt almost apologetic for being the way that she was.

If you have ever felt the need to apologise for who you are, I urge you to STOP. It's time to say NO MORE to the mismatch between the woman you portray and the woman that you really are. It's time to RID YOURSELF of the stress and pressure of trying to be someone that you're not. It's time to REGAIN sight of who you really are and STOP conforming to other people's expectations of you.

3 | *Common Internal Challenges*

There are common internal challenges that I frequently see amongst the introverted women leaders that I work with. These are self-doubt, imposter syndrome and perfectionism. These issues are not exclusive to those who identify as introverted, nor are they exclusive to women. I coach extroverted women and men who also struggle with these challenges. Likewise, it is not all introverted women who experience them. However, because this book is for introverted women, and I see these issues frequently with introverted women that I work with, I am addressing them from the perspective of their experiences.

Often these issues stem from their childhood experiences, or situations they have been in during their early career. Add to that the misconceptions about introversion and the dominant extroverted culture, and for many of these women, this compounds these issues for them. Whilst there is little research available regarding how these issues impact introverted women, from my personal experience, and that of my clients, they are less prevalent for those who are introvert and proud. Namely, secure within themselves about being introverted.

Often when coaching introverted women who experience these issues, once they have accepted that it is ok to be introverted, and they are being true to their authentic self, these issues dissipate and are no longer a challenge for them. Whilst I had problems finding research that backed up what I've found in my work, there is available research that shows what impact being a minority, or not fitting the cultural norm, has on a person's view of themselves. I address each of the three issues separately, with examples and exercises so you can see how it may apply to you and what you can do about it.

SELF-DOUBT

The responses to my survey amongst introverted women who are senior leaders showed that for 73% of them self-doubt was an issue. As previously mentioned, self-doubt is not exclusive to introverts, and there may well be equal numbers of extroverted women leaders who have issues with this, as well as men. Many introverted women leaders have grown up in environments that value extroversion over introversion, causing some to believe that they are not good enough. This can make it challenging for them when their preferred way of being is totally different to their colleagues at the table.

An element of self-doubt is not actually a bad thing. It is when we let it debilitate us or let it negatively hinder our performance that it becomes a problem. Without some self-doubt we could become overconfident, arrogant and lacking humility. Whilst confidence is good, when it swings over to arrogance and pig-headedness, these are not good traits to see in a leader. Having a healthy dose of self-doubt, coupled with humility, are good qualities to have as a leader. It means that you are open to listening and learning from others. It means that you don't become arrogant thinking you are better than everyone else.

For some introverted women who are leaders, self-doubt can negatively eat away at them, preventing them from achieving optimal performance. This can be even more so if they are in a predominately extroverted, male environment and have had to work hard to smash their way through the corporate glass ceiling. Not only is she faced with the challenges that being a woman in such senior environments brings, add introversion to the mix and it can cause an internal suffocation of her expressing her true self. In her mind, she doubts whether she is worthy or whether she is good enough. Looking at her colleagues, but because she's not like them, she thinks that the problem lies with her. If she's not careful, over time she loses sight of her strengths. She focuses entirely on her weaknesses, exacerbating what she can't do, what she doesn't do, and only making herself feel worse in the process.

When we focus on our perceived faults, if we're not careful, that is all we ever see in ourselves. We distort and magnify them, letting them take up too much space in our head. For the introverted woman leader with self-doubt, my question to you is: why are you doubting yourself? It is no accident that you are in the position that you are in. It is not luck that got you there either. You got to where you are because someone recognised your talents. Someone believed that you are good at what you do. And someone was confident that you were the best person for the role. If only you could see that for yourself!

What we think and believe about ourselves becomes our reality. For many of us, if we think and believe we are not good enough, or we doubt ourselves, it doesn't make us feel good about ourselves or our capabilities. If we allow them to, we let our emotions take over, acting and behaving according to how we feel. And when you're a busy, introverted woman leader with self-doubt, your emotions may be causing you to think negatively about yourself. We are very much led by our emotions, acting and behaving according to how we're feeling. When we think negatively about ourselves and doubt ourselves, it can make us feel anxious, fearful or lacking in confidence. As a result, we don't do what we want to do or need to do. Or, we do what needs to be done, but because of the self-doubt and how we are feeling, we don't do it to the best of our ability.

These women are amazingly talented but put a lot of pressure on themselves with the overthinking they do about their ability to do their work. Take my friend, herself a high-achieving woman and for privacy reasons, let's call her Diane. She is a talented writer and has written some pretty good stuff. She has written her own book and contributed to two others. Prior to publishing her book, she once wrote a blog about a matter that was headline news and asked her partner, himself a published author, for feedback on it.

He critiqued it and made a number of suggestions to change it which left Diane feeling completely deflated and discouraged about her efforts. Prior to showing it to her partner, Diane's gut feeling was that she was happy with it and felt confident about what she had written. These negative comments, whilst done in a supportive way, had the effect of causing Diane to doubt her writing ability. How many times has that happened to you? You've produced a piece of work, felt confident about it, only to have someone make a negative comment that knocks the wind out of your self-confidence. As a result of this self-doubt, Diane questioned whether she was really any good as a writer. She started ruminating over things, thinking that because she has to put so much thought and effort into her writing and because writing for her doesn't flow as it does for her partner, there must be something wrong with her.

Overthinking can kill your creativity and ability to get in to flow with the work that you are doing. Overthinking and questioning whether your work is really any good, or thinking that you are a fraud and trying to make sure your work is absolutely perfect, puts you under a lot of strain. That pressure can cause you to feel anxious and if you are led by your emotions, it is more likely that you will act irrationally about what it is that you need to do. What Diane decided to do was to make the changes her partner had suggested, which risked losing the tone of her authentic voice in the article. Having made these changes, she then got feedback from another friend whose feedback was similar to her partner's, causing even more confusion and self-doubt. Recognising that she had spent far too long agonising over the article, she decided to go with what she originally wrote (plus a few minor amendments) and she published it. And guess what – she got great reviews!

Diane was initially going to go with her gut instinct and publish the article but she let the views of others persuade her otherwise, causing her to doubt herself and overthink. How often do you ignore the gut instinct that is telling you something is the right thing for you to do? How often do you listen to the opinion of others, let their views knock your confidence and then procrastinate, delaying completing your project or piece of work because you don't believe your work is good enough? Diane had a track record of producing quality written work but because of the self-limiting beliefs she held about her writing, she would overthink and block her creativity.

When these moments of self-doubt and feeling like a fraud arise, stop and rationalise your thoughts and beliefs about your situation and put things into perspective. Remind yourself of why it is that you are in the role. Make a list of your major successes to date.

I am sure that there have been many times in your life when you doubted yourself and your ability, but you went ahead and did it anyway, and everything turned out ok. Think back to those times. What was it that got you through? What skills and strengths did you draw on? Who supported you? What can you learn from those previous experiences and apply to your situation now?

The delay in getting her article out meant that Diane's post was no longer timely – that particular news headline was now history. Although the subject matter she wrote about was still very much relevant, delaying publishing it in a timely manner was a missed opportunity for her. Missing out on all the attention it was likely to have received off the back of the news headlines. Diane compared herself to her partner, a well-versed, published author, and in her eyes saw that she was not as good as him. But Diane is Diane; she is not her partner. The audience Diane writes for is not the same as her partner's audience. Just like you are you, and comparing yourself to others and putting yourself down in the process only feeds into the self-doubt that you have.

Do you see yourself in Diane, missing out on opportunities because self-doubt is causing you to delay? Do you doubt your ability? Remember, you didn't get to where you are by luck. It didn't just happen by chance that you have achieved all you have to date. I'm sure you got to where you are because you put time and effort in. You honed your knowledge and skills and put them to good use. You got to where you are because you are good at what you do. That is why you are doing the role and not someone else.

If you could wave a magic wand and self-doubt was no longer an issue for you, what would it be like? Would you let people talk and walk over you? Would you take bold and courageous action? Would you not be too concerned if people disagreed with you, or criticised your work or point of view? Imagine a life where you didn't let self-doubt have such a negative hold. What is the difference that it would make? Learning how to rationalise your situation and put things into perspective will help you to change how you feel. If you change how you feel, you change how you act and behave.

When you doubt yourself and your abilities, are you just focusing on the things that you're not good at to the exclusion of everything else? If so, is that an accurate representation of who you really are? With 23 grand slam titles to her name (and 8 runner-ups), you could look at tennis player Serena Williams and think she is the ultimate tennis playing machine. But just like everyone else, she has her weaknesses too. It has been said that the baseline is her weakness. But does she focus on that, magnifying it in her mind? Has she let that prevent her from achieving optimal performance? What do you think her results over the years would have been like if she had?

In order to change how you feel about yourself, you need to change how you think and what you believe about yourself. You need to challenge your thoughts and beliefs, look for the evidence to support them, rationalise them and put things into perspective. My client Debbie wanted to go for a senior leadership role, but she doubted her ability to speak up confidently at meetings, which would be a big aspect of the senior role. Because she doubted herself, it affected her self-confidence. I will address speaking up and being heard in chapter 4, but for now, will just focus on the self-doubt element.

It turned out that in a voluntary capacity, Debbie was the Chair of a large charity, and had no problems speaking at meetings. She even spoke at their annual conference in front of 100s of people. She found speaking up in her voluntary capacity to not be a problem. It was only when it came to paid roles that she had the issue. Using cognitive behavioural coaching (an approach I find works well with my clients who have self-limiting beliefs), I helped her to explore her thoughts and beliefs about what would happen if she was to do public speaking in her paid role.

When we are faced with uncertainty or have to do something we are fearful of, we often imagine the worst possible outcome, and this was the case with Debbie. She believed that she would make a fool of herself and be ridiculed. I challenged her thoughts and beliefs about this and asked her where the evidence was to support her belief. Using the example of her voluntary role, I asked her when she had ever made a fool of herself and been ridiculed. Through coaching, she was able to recognise that her self-doubt came from an experience in her early career 20 years before. She had been the only woman in a meeting and was made to feel that her point of view didn't count, and that she never had anything good to say. At such a young and impressionable age, this affected the way she viewed herself going forward, doubting herself and wondering whether she really was any good. She found it easier to do public speaking in her voluntary role as Chair because she wasn't being paid for it. Whereas in her paid, employed roles, she had a limiting belief as to whether she was good enough to be paid, based on that early career experience.

Once she realised this, she recognised that she was actually a good public speaker, and spoke well chairing the Trustee Board meetings. Otherwise she wouldn't have been voted in as Chair and asked to address the audience at the conference. She was also able to see that the behaviour of those men would be totally unacceptable today, and not only that, other women in the organisation had had a similar experience. She could now see that the issue didn't lie with her, but with the men who had treated her so unfairly. By challenging her thinking, she was able to see that the reality of the meetings she attended in paid employment was not really as bad as she perceived. This shift in perception changed how she felt, and as a result she overcame the fear and self-doubt.

If after reading this you are still doubting yourself, try the exercise below.

SELF-DOUBT EXERCISE

In order to stop doubting yourself and to develop belief in yourself and your abilities, you need to change the beliefs you hold about yourself. This is more than just thinking positive or doing positive affirmations. It's about examining your belief, challenging it and disputing it and changing it for something more helpful. Ask yourself the following questions, and write down your answers to each of them in your journal.

- What is the area(s) in which you doubt yourself and your ability, or lack self-belief?
- Where does this belief come from?
- What were the circumstances in which this belief arose?
- What could have been going on at the time to cause you to develop this belief, and what relevance does it have today?
- How do you know this belief is true? What evidence is there to support it?
- Looking back over your career and life, how many times has what you believed come about?
- If what you believe is going to happen was to happen, what could you do?
- How is holding on to this belief helping you?
- What would be a more helpful belief for you to hold going forward?
- What will you do differently going forward, as a result of doing this exercise?
- What can you do if the self-doubt starts to creep in again?

On a scale of 1 to 10 (where 1 is not confident at all and 10 is yes, I'm on this and I'm very confident), where would you rate yourself in terms of confidence to do what you say you will do differently?

If you rated yourself less than an 8, what needs to happen to raise it a point or two?

Whenever you find yourself in a situation where there is something you need to do or you want to do and you are doubting yourself, pause for a moment and examine what is going on in your mind. Challenge your thoughts and beliefs, write them down if possible and then write down corresponding thoughts which are more helpful for you. As mentioned, we are very much led by our emotions and act and behave according to how we are feeling. If you can capture those unhelpful thoughts as and when they happen, it will help you to change how you feel.

We often notice the physiological symptoms from feeling anxious before we notice what is going on in our mind. For some people it's a tight knot in their stomach, or tension in their neck, shoulder or head. For some their heart starts beating faster, for some they go red. Where does it show up in you? Next time you need or want to do something and you are doubting yourself, and you notice that physiological symptom, pause and do what I describe above. The more you practise this, it will increase your self-awareness, making it easier for you to recognise when YOU are getting in the way of your own progress.

IMPOSTER SYNDROME

'Imposter syndrome can be defined as a collection of feelings of inadequacy that persist despite evident success. 'Imposters' suffer from chronic self-doubt and a sense of intellectual fraudulence that override any feelings of success or external proof of their competence. They seem unable to internalize their accomplishments, however successful they are in their field. High achieving, highly successful people often suffer, so imposter syndrome doesn't equate with low self-esteem or a lack of self-confidence. In fact, some researchers have linked it with perfectionism, especially in women and among academics.' Gill Corkindale[1]

Having achieved a senior position in an environment where you are 'different' can contribute to the introverted woman wondering how on earth she got the role. Telling herself that one day she's going to get found out and they're going to realise that they made a mistake. According to Psychology Magazine, 70% of people (this includes men as well as women, and extroverts as well as introverts) experience 'imposter syndrome'[2]. Pauline R. Clance and Suzanne Imes, who coined the phrase Imposter Syndrome in 1978, identified that there were two types of situations from which it arose. Both occurred in childhood – the first one is where the individual was made to feel like they weren't as good as their siblings or other children. The second situation is being put on a pedestal as the perfect child who could do no wrong and a feeling that you can't live up to the expected ideals of others[3].

My client Frances experienced imposter syndrome when she initially came to me for coaching. She had a senior position but didn't recognise that she got it through her own merit. Because she had always been the 'good' one as a child, without knowing it her mum and sister had labelled her the 'golden child' who could do no wrong. Even as an adult, they put her on a pedestal, which was something she found hard to live up to.

Imposter syndrome is something that I often see affecting high-achieving introverted women. Feeling like a fraud; waiting with bated breath for the corporate fraud police to suss them out. In a survey of high-achieving introverted senior women I conducted, 53% of them identified themselves as experiencing imposter syndrome. In an extroverted environment where colleagues are more gregarious, speak up more at meetings, and get more attention, if you have not yet accepted that introversion is a strength (and still view your introverted traits as a weakness), it is easy to compare yourself to those who get all the attention and think that you are the one that shouldn't be there. Add to that the fact that you have been given such a big role, and there may be aspects about the role you find challenging, this sometimes makes you feel like a fish out of water. Is it any wonder you feel like a fraud and doubt your ability to do the role?

Studies suggest that those who are in the minority are more susceptible to imposter syndrome[4]. When you are different to the majority in an organisation, whether it be gender, race, sexual orientation, or another characteristic such as being introverted in an extroverted environment, because you are different, it can make you feel like you are a fraud. Also, you may find that the more senior you get and the more responsibility you have (particularly if you achieved this over a short space of time), the more the imposter is evoked in you.

As mentioned, men also experience this and an example of a man who has been open about it is Howard Schultz, the former CEO of Starbucks. He is reported to have admitted to having experienced it, and is quoted in the *New York Times* as saying, *"Very few people, whether you've been in that job before or not, get into the seat and believe today that they are now qualified to be the CEO. They're not going to tell you that, but it's true..."*[5] However, in my experience, men are less likely to be open about it than women, but senior people openly talking about their challenges, as Howard Schultz did, removes the stigma associated with it. This can help people to see that they're not the only ones experiencing such challenges, and has the ability to diminish what may have been an overly magnified issue.

It can also rear its head if someone is of a different socio-economic background to the majority. My client Jeff was in his early thirties and on track for a senior leadership role within the organisation where he worked. As a black, introverted man who went to a university that was lower in the league table rankings, he felt out of place in meetings. They tended to be full of white, middle-aged, Oxbridge-educated men, with whom he had little in common. Because of this, he would often clam up in meetings and found it difficult to speak up, believing that he would get found out that he didn't have anything good to say. Once he was able to recognise his strengths and accept himself as he was, as well as applying techniques from chapter 4, he saw his confidence levels soar and he was able to overcome the imposter syndrome.

As an introverted woman in an extroverted environment, if you don't fit the mould, it can certainly feel as if you are different. Comparing yourself to others, putting yourself down in the process, thinking that you're a fraud and that you are going to get found out. Over time the effects of Imposter Syndrome can cause stress and emotional issues; it can even lead to depression. Having been promoted to Director position, Susie was wondering why they had given her the role. She hadn't been in the organisation as long as the majority of her colleagues. Not only was she an introvert, she originated from another country, and had an accent that was different to everyone else's. She felt that she was very different to her peers. She didn't think that she was performing to the best of her ability, despite there being no evidence to support that belief.

She compared herself to her extroverted colleague who talked non-stop at meetings, always expressing their opinion and having something to say. She not only found it hard to fit in, she doubted her ability to do the role, and was very stressed as a result. When I challenged her thinking on her comparison to her colleague, she saw that her colleague talked far too much, and on reflection, she didn't want to be like that. Looking at her skills, her strengths and what she was good at, she was finally able to see why she had been given the role. Imposter syndrome is something I often see in high-achieving women that causes them to self-doubt, to procrastinate, to strive for perfection and delay. It stops them from seizing the moment and they miss out on opportunities. It puts them under a lot of pressure and holds them back from being all that they are capable of being.

After getting three promotions over a relatively short period of time, I myself became a victim of imposter syndrome (although I didn't know there was a name for what I was experiencing at the time). I found myself in this much bigger role and initially kept thinking to myself 'they're going to realise they've made a mistake and shouldn't have given me the promotion'. I was half expecting to get that email or that phone call informing me 'Carol, we're really sorry but...'. However, because of the work that I had done on my self-development over the years, I quickly realised that I was self-sabotaging. I told myself that I went through a fair and open recruitment process and was deemed to be the best person for the role. I told myself that if they believed that I could do the role, I needed to believe it myself.

I set about identifying what it was that caused me to doubt my ability to carry out the role. I went through every aspect of what was required of me and identified two areas which I found challenging. These were my financial responsibilities and health and safety responsibilities. I was now a budget holder and had all the responsibilities that came with that – something that I had never experienced before. I also now had health and safety responsibility for four buildings, the hundreds of people that worked in them and the hundreds of people that passed through the doors each and every day. At a health and safety training event to go through responsibilities under the Corporate Homicide Act 2007 when it was introduced, I was told that I had overall responsibility under the Act. I was told that I was responsible for all the contractors that came on site, and if there were any fatalities, it could result in me facing a corporate manslaughter charge if I hadn't ensured certain things were in place. No pressure!

Once I had narrowed it down and saw that out of the many requirements of the role (and believe me, there were a lot) there were only two elements that I found challenging, I was able to get the necessary training. I was able to bring myself up to speed and feel confident doing what was expected of me, rather than feeling like a fraud, waiting to get caught out. Years later, I now help women who experience the same issue. They feel like a fraud and believe that they're going to get found out, experiencing the stress and anxiety that this can cause them.

For many of them, whilst it may be different circumstances and different environments, their story is similar to mine. If you are experiencing imposter syndrome and feel like a fraud, remind yourself of why you got the role that you do. It wasn't luck. I'm sure it wasn't because someone felt sorry for you. And it most certainly wasn't the case that you were not good at what you do. You got the role because you demonstrated that you have the skills and ability to do it and that you were the best person for it. In her book *Her Way to the Top*, Hira Ali suggests doing a brain dump and writing everything down so that you can separate the emotion from the facts[6].

If you're still not convinced, have a go at the two exercises below:

Exercise 1 – Whom have you fooled?[7]

Make a list of all the people you have fooled, and write a letter telling them how you have fooled them. Don't give them the letter – it's for your purposes only! If I use my own situation which I described above, I would write to the three people on my interview panel and it would read something like this:

Dear XXX, XXX, XXX

I am sorry to have to write and tell you but you should never have given me the job. I fooled you all into believing that I could do it. I am not really good enough for the role, and I am not quite sure how I managed to convince you that I was.

Yours sincerely

Carol

Then, imagine what their response would be, and write it down. Again, using my situation as an example, this is the sort of reply that I could imagine they would send.

> *Dear Carol*
>
> *Thank you for your letter, which we are very surprised to receive from you. We use a tried and tested process when conducting interviews, which we apply to ALL interview candidates, as was the case in your situation. We only appoint people on merit. Based on your responses to our questions, and your presentation, you were by far the best candidate for the role.*
>
> *You either must think that we are stupid and have no experience whatsoever of conducting interviews and making a selection or you are a fantastic liar, and lied throughout the whole interview.*
>
> *Yours sincerely*
>
> *The Interview Panel*

When doing this exercise, use factual evidence, and separate the facts from your feelings. In my situation, my feelings were that I was not really good enough to do the role. The facts were that people are appointed on being able to demonstrate their ability to do the role.

Exercise 2 – Revisit your job description

Dig out your job description and use it as a checklist for all the things that are required of you in your role. Put a tick by the ones which you are confident in doing and a cross by the ones you are not.

With the things you are not confident in, what do you need to bring yourself up to speed, and who can support you?

PERFECTIONISM

I liken the introverted female leader who is also a perfectionist to a swan. Gliding along the river, whilst underneath frantically paddling away. Smooth and graceful on the outside, but for the perfectionist leader, beneath the surface, her levels of anxiety swing up and down because of those perfectionist tendencies. A lot of this is self-inflicted, arising from the undue pressure to be perfect that she constantly puts on herself.

A fear of failure because they are not good enough is often at the root of perfectionist behaviour. Not all introverted women are perfectionists and extroverts can be perfectionists too. In my survey of senior introverted women, 53% said they were perfectionists. Perfectionism often arises as a result of wanting to achieve success whilst having a fear of failure.

If you are an introverted leader and a perfectionist, ask yourself what impact constantly striving for perfection is having on you. Not only that, if you have perfectionist expectations of your teams, stop and think whether you are putting excessive pressure on them, expecting them to meet your unattainable standard. You may procrastinate a lot, not moving forward, waiting for conditions to be perfect before you take action. Or, you may delay completing tasks because you worry that you won't be able to complete them perfectly.

Because you are so risk averse, you may find that you get left behind. Being a perfectionist can be stressful. Working excessive hours, ruminating over tasks and projects, spending far too long completing them and striving for a standard far higher than excellence. Whilst it is good to strive for excellence in what you do, that constant striving for perfectionism will eventually take its toll. By constantly aiming for perfection, you are making things much more stressful than they need to be. Perfectionism can lead to procrastination, stress and anxiety, risk-aversion, and not moving forward; it can cause difficulty in making decisions, and it affects your effectiveness as a leader. Finally, it can lead to depression.

It may be that you are an inward perfectionist and find yourself questioning whether you are good enough. Or you may be an outward perfectionist in that other people don't live up to your high standards, and your teams walk around on eggshells, trying to live up to the impossible standards you expect of them.

Sheila was an inward perfectionist and she would often work late making sure that her work was completed to perfection before submitting it. She was self-critical, despite always getting great reviews in her performance appraisals, and had a fear of failure. When I asked her what she had failed at in her career, she struggled to think of something. No one had ever criticised her work, or told her that it needed to be perfect. This way of being was stressful for her. She would often feel deflated after putting so much effort and energy into a project, only to receive a casual response when she delivered.

Whilst Sheila knew the pressure she had put herself under to complete it, no one else was aware of the extra hours and ruminating that had gone into her trying to make it perfect. They only saw the end result and that she had delivered what was required. During her coaching sessions, it transpired that as a child she had been told she would not amount to anything. Without realising it, the lasting effect of this was perfectionism and putting herself under immense pressure so that people would think that she was good enough.

First of all, I got Sheila to do the exercise from the previous chapter on self-acceptance. I then got her to do the exercise above on self-doubt. She then set about raising her tolerance levels so that she wouldn't put so much pressure on herself. Rather than working late and going over and over a project she needed to deliver, she drew the line when it met the standard required. Even though she knew that it wasn't to her usual levels of perfection, no one else even noticed. The difference in her stress levels was immense. This was the first time that she could recall delivering on a project and not feeling stressed about it.

Helping Sheila to raise her tolerance levels in this way, to accept that she was good enough and to recognise she didn't have to own the label that others had put on her, helped her to manage perfectionism and be more confident about her abilities.

Elizabeth was an outward perfectionist who had a very high expectation of her team. Because she set such a high expectation for herself and was able to achieve it, she gave her team little praise when they did achieve the high bar she set. To her they were only doing their jobs and what was expected of them. It transpired that growing up, she was deemed the perfect child and was put on a pedestal because she was an over-achiever. Even as an adult, her family still had her on this pedestal.

The downside of this was that she put a lot of pressure on herself to maintain this attitude, and she also had a high expectation (often unrealistic) of others and she found it stressful when they did not achieve the levels of perfection she expected. She also experienced imposter syndrome, which often goes hand in hand with perfectionism. Her lack of self-awareness meant that she was unable to see the impact her behaviour was having on her team.

Challenging her thoughts and beliefs during our coaching sessions increased her self-awareness and so she was able to see the pressure she put her team under. She raised her tolerance levels as a result of learning to recognise that they were doing their best and to the standard the organisation expected. She identified how to get the best from her team and started praising them for a job well done (something she never felt the need to do previously). She set regular one-to-one meetings with them and adopted a coaching approach at these meetings, rather than talking at them. Because this was something that she was not used to, she initially found it uncomfortable. However, she saw the benefits of being able to adapt her style in order to get the best out of a situation and create win/win situations for her and her team.

As an introverted perfectionist, you may come across as aloof, distant and a bit of an ice queen. Other people only see the swan-like appearance that you exude, oblivious to the internal struggle going on underneath. Self-acceptance, increasing your tolerance levels and recognising that your best IS good enough, will ease the pressure that you put on yourself. You may find this hard to do at first and you may find it difficult to let things go, but I challenge you to try it (doing it in small steps if necessary) and see just how good it can feel!

Perfectionism can hinder your personal effectiveness as a leader if you let it, and addressing it is within your control.

> 'Farmers who wait for perfect weather never plant. If they watch every cloud, they never harvest.'
>
> Ecclesiastes 11:4

SELF-REFLECTION EXERCISE

- In what way do self-limiting beliefs, self-doubt, imposter syndrome or perfectionism hold you back?
- If you are a perfectionist, what can you do to accept that good is good enough and raise your tolerance levels?
- What will it be like for you when you overcome these self-limiting beliefs?
- What can you do to make this happen?

CHAPTER

4 | *Speaking Up and Being Heard*

'**Y**ou need to speak up more.' 'You need to be more vocal.' 'You're too quiet.' These are some of the things my clients often tell me they get told when they first come to me for coaching. One of my managers used to tell me that I needed to speak up more about my achievements in the Area leadership meetings, but I preferred to let the results speak for themselves. However, whilst this is my preferred way of being, I recognise that in the 'noisy' world of work, speaking up and telling those who need to know about our achievements is necessary if we want to be seen, be heard and stand out. It is something that I have had to work on, even more so since starting my business as the 'noise' is even louder in the small business world as everybody is self-promoting. In chapter 6 I cover ways in which you can self-promote that feel more natural to the introverted woman.

Speaking up at meetings and being heard is something that many introverted women find challenging. For some it is because they also lack confidence at speaking up in front of a group, but for others, it is because many corporate meetings are conducted in a way that tends to better suit those who are extroverted. With a focus on people responding on the spot, and louder personalities dominating the floor, they don't allow for the thinking and reflecting that is typical of introverts before they speak out.

Do you sit in your leadership team meetings observing and reflecting as introverts do? Only speaking when you have something valuable to contribute? Not just speaking for speaking's sake. Do people question why you are even there because they think you don't have much to say? Unfortunately, the way that many leadership team meetings are held does not play to the introverted leader's strengths. They are often a lot of buzz, lots of talk, with people firing off responses having given little reflective thought. Whilst these meetings may get results, they may have missed out on the valuable contributions of everyone that is present, all because they are not set up to engage with everyone in the best possible way.

This chapter will first of all look at how you, as an introverted woman, can speak up confidently and assertively at meetings, and be heard. Addressing any self-limiting beliefs, preparation, positioning yourself, and tone of voice are some of the things we will cover. Then we will look at strategies for how you can make meetings more inclusive for introverts if you are in a position to change (or influence change) the way your meetings are conducted. Sprinkled throughout this chapter you will see the words that readers of my articles have shared with me about their experiences or what they have observed about introverts speaking up in meetings.

> 'Everyone's voice matters and often the most impactful messages that can make a difference are never heard because of over-bearing leaders speaking above others making it uncomfortable for some to express their comments. Your post is another great example of making sure teams encourage and empower others.' Mario

Studies have found that women (more so than men) find their voices go unheard in meetings. In a *New York Times* article, Sheryl Sandberg and Adam Grant wrote that when a woman speaks in a professional setting, she is barely heard, or deemed aggressive[1]. One study found that a female CEO who talked immensely longer than others in an organisational environment was considered less competent and less suitable for leadership than a male CEO who talked for just as long. This view was held by both men and women, and shows that there are both men and women who hold certain unhelpful beliefs about gender hierarchies.[2] The same study also found that a female CEO who didn't talk a lot and didn't talk with great energy and enthusiasm (namely she had low volubility) was just as competent and worthy of leadership as a male CEO with high volubility. Whereas a male CEO with less volubility was perceived as being less competent and less suitable for leadership.

If this study is anything to go by, for the introverted woman leader who strives to speak up and be heard, it is not just a case of speaking more, it is about having the ability to speak up and get her message heard in a way that is influential and impactful. With the gender stereotypes around volubility, the introverted woman needs to not only contend with being deemed aggressive or barely heard when she speaks in a professional setting, she also has to contend with meetings not being geared towards getting her to perform at her best.

DON'T LET THE FEAR OF SPEAKING UP CONSUME YOUR THOUGHTS

When it comes to speaking up and being heard, it is necessary to separate the emotion from the fact. As discussed in chapter 3, we are very much led by our emotions and many of us act and behave according to how we are feeling. This often is as a result of the thoughts and beliefs we hold about ourselves, our situations and our environments. Often those thoughts and beliefs are unhelpful and can be irrational, as can be the case with your thoughts and beliefs about you speaking up and being heard in meetings. If you feel tense and anxious about speaking up, that will come across in how you communicate. Being stressed will hinder you from speaking fluently and concisely.[3] In particular, if you want to be heard and get people to buy in to what you have to say, you have to be able to portray the right level of assertiveness and politeness in order to maximise people taking on board what you are saying. In order to make it easier for you to speak up and be heard, it will help if you can identify whether it is a case of you holding self-limiting beliefs about yourself, or whether it is the way meetings are conducted that doesn't play to your strengths.

Annette would get so anxious about meetings that she often kept quiet, even though she knew there was no substance to what was being said in meetings. Working in a male-dominated environment, she was usually the only woman at meetings. The CEO would always go to her male colleague with whom she worked quite closely, even though she was the one who did most of the 'hard' work. She recognised that if she was to be taken seriously and get the recognition that she deserved, she needed to change her narrative. She put into practice the techniques I share with you in this chapter, and she found that people started to listen to her during meetings, but not only that, it was as if the CEO started to see her and all that she was capable of for the first time.

Because firing off responses on the spot may not be your natural style, you may worry about having to give an immediate response, and imagine all kinds of things going wrong. This will then cause you to feel anxious about speaking. Because you're worrying and feeling anxious, you may either not speak up, or if you do speak up, because you are anxious the words don't come out as you want them to. You may find that when you think about it, or when you're in the meeting or about to go in, you get a knot in your stomach, or that tension in your neck, shoulders or head (or wherever it shows up physiologically for you) starts to build up.

When you notice the physiological symptoms, capture the thoughts that are going through your mind. These thoughts are contributing to you feeling anxious and aren't helping you. Challenge your thoughts and beliefs and change them to something that is helpful, such as the value your contribution will add to the conversation.

If you're in the middle of a meeting and you don't have time to do this, tell yourself that you haven't got time to worry about speaking up now. Remind yourself that right now the important thing for you to focus on is that the message you want to deliver is heard. Tell yourself that you will go through your worries at the end of the day at a particular time, but right now your focus is making your valuable input to this discussion. Chances are by the end of the day it will no longer be an issue because you did it, you spoke up and everything was ok.

What is the reason why you find it difficult speaking up? What is the reason why your voice goes unheard? English was not the first language for Elsbeth, and she struggled with speaking up and voicing her opinion at leadership meetings. She believed that because of her accent, and because English was not her first language, people didn't understand her, and that she didn't come across articulately and confidently. Because of this belief, she invariably remained quiet in meetings and she lacked confidence about speaking up. When I challenged her thinking and her beliefs, it turned out that no one had ever told her that they couldn't understand her. Neither had anyone ever questioned her articulacy.

She was able to see that in the event that someone did indicate that they didn't understand her, she could repeat herself and get clarification that they understood. Furthermore, as she was not British born and English was not her first language, it was inevitable that she would have an accent, and that was ok. Not to add that she was fluent in five different languages, whereas the majority of her colleagues could only speak one! This helped to change Elsbeth's perspective about herself in meetings and helped her to be more confident. What about you? If you still find that you have self-limiting beliefs about how you perform in meetings, do the exercise in Chapter 3 and apply it to how you feel about meetings.

DO YOUR THINKING AND REFLECTING BEFOREHAND

As introverts, we tend to prefer observing and reflecting on what is being discussed and then coming forward with a valuable contribution. Unfortunately, the style of many leadership meetings does not allow for this reflection to take place. We are expected to give a response there and then. It is often this being put on the spot, without having time to think, that has been challenging for the introverted women I have worked with. Preparing yourself for the meeting in advance can go a long way in helping you to speak up. Go through the agenda in advance of the meeting, and reflect on the items that are listed. What are your thoughts about them? What views do you have about what is being suggested? Make notes on what your thoughts are, and any ideas or solutions that you have, so that when the item is discussed at the meeting, you will already have formed some opinions and can put those forward. If you have any ideas or suggestions for the meeting, think about what possible objections there may be. What are your responses to the possible objections? Find out in advance what colleagues think about topics that are to be discussed so you are able to come up with possible responses to different points of view.

Maria would get quite stressed before meetings with a particular stakeholder. She knew that they would be challenging with on-the-spot questions thrown at her, and she worried she would make a fool of herself. As a result, she didn't feel confident going in to these meetings. Doing her preparation in advance and anticipating possible objections meant that she felt fully prepared. She was then able to go to these meetings stress free and feeling confident.

GET TO KNOW THE OTHERS
WHO WILL BE ATTENDING

If you find walking into a meeting full of strangers and asserting yourself challenging, familiarise yourself with the people you don't know by connecting with them beforehand. You could do this on LinkedIn, by sending them a connection request with a note to say that you are both due to attend such and such meeting, and it would be good to connect here on LinkedIn. Or drop them an introductory email. By having an exchange of conversations before the meeting, you will go into the meeting having made the unfamiliar more familiar, making it more comfortable for you. Arrange to arrive at your meetings early so that as people arrive, you can start to engage in conversation with them.

A lot of knowledge and information is shared at meetings. A network that is built on close personal relationships is more likely to foster trust and loyalty, which are motivators for knowledge sharing. Introverts are typically good at developing and maintaining close personal relationships, so develop personal relationships with those you regularly meet with. This will make it easier for you to speak up and share information.

'It's also sometimes helpful to recognise there are other ways of contributing to a meeting beyond making the thoroughly considered 'killer point'. For instance, supporting another's viewpoint, making a connection between points of discussion, asking a question.' David P

THINK ABOUT HOW YOU POSITION YOURSELF

If there is any one person in particular that you want to be heard by, sit facing them if you are able to. It is said that sitting face to face makes for better interaction with those you are talking to, whereas sitting side by side involves mutual orientation toward some third party or object[4]. In a meeting where louder personalities are vying for the limelight, you may find it difficult to get a word in. There are vocal and body movement techniques that you can adopt, which will help you to get the attention of the room and get your point heard.

When you have something to say, start to prepare yourself before the current person finishes speaking. Be attentive to the signs that they are nearing the end of what they have to say. Hold your gaze on the person speaking and lean forward. As they finish what they have to say, jump in and say your piece[5].

'Introverts can gain quiet respect without saying much – an example I was in a regular meeting with a rich guy who used to shout and get red-faced – going into long annoying and time-wasting rants which we used to just tolerate – one day after a particular such outburst he finished and turned to me beside him and said to me 'do you agree?' I simply said 'sorry – when you start shouting I stop listening' WELL! – his face went bright red – a sharp intake of breath – the rest of the room hung in fear and suspense – he was about to explode but said nothing and just managed to contain himself! Ever since that day he no longer shouts in our regular meetings.' David G

When a speaker looks at the person they are speaking to, it can be seen that they are speaking to that individual. Likewise, if the person being spoken to gazes back at the speaker, it appears as though they are listening[6]. Get the attention of the person/persons you want to hear your message so that they are gazing at you. You don't want to be speaking and realise that the people you want to hear what you have to say are not paying attention to you. When you start speaking, you may not yet have the attention of the others in the meeting. As people hear you and start to pay you attention, restart what it is that you want to say. An alternative to restarting what you were saying is to pause. Pause for long enough so that it is noticed but not too long that people think you have finished speaking and for someone else to jump in.

Your tone of voice will help in how your message is heard and received. When speaking, be clear, be concise, and be assertive. If someone tries to cut in before you have finished speaking, state firmly and calmly that you have not finished yet.

> 'My mentor is an introvert. I have watched her a number of times, listening to ideas and then jotting a message or note during a meeting and handing it to the facilitator at a break or on the way out. Because her input is often more well thought out and written in sentences, not just phrases shouted out, often her ideas communicated in the note end up being included in a final draft. In this way she is MORE effective because of her communication style.' Denise

Many introverts don't like to be put on the spot and be required to give a response without having had time to think and reflect. I was once at a meeting that was being chaired by a very extroverted woman. There was an ongoing discussion and she suddenly directed her attention to a man who was quiet, and sharply said, 'What do you think?' This put the man in an awkward position and I could sense his distaste at being thrust into the limelight like that and being expected to respond on the spot. He looked very uncomfortable, and as a result, he stammered out that he had nothing further to add.

If you find that this happens to you and you're at a loss as to what to say, buy yourself some time. Give your initial thoughts on what is being discussed, and let people know that once you have had a chance to reflect on the issue, if you have anything further to add, you will let them know. If there is an issue that you want to contribute a response to but need to reflect on your thoughts, make it known that you think there are some interesting points being raised and you have some thoughts on the issue and would like to come back to it. This will give you time to reflect and gather your thoughts together, enabling you to make a considered response.

> *'Another technique I've found quite useful is the open-ended question – it buys you time while maintaining awareness of your engagement.'* Nancy

Speak up early in meetings. Not only do you get it out of the way, but you also get to say something before the meeting gets into full flow, where questions and responses are being fired across the table.

> 'Get stuck in early in a meeting and find your voice. Once you've been heard once, it's much easier for people to listen next time.' Angus

As introverts, we are well known for our listening skills, and meetings are a great place for you to flex your listening muscles. Listen to what is being said (as well as to what is not said) and ask thought-provoking questions.

> 'Early in my career, I was told by a mentor: "If you were invited to a meeting, your voice is meant to be heard. If I had no interest in your opinion, I would not have included you." This changed my thinking about speaking up, for the better. Hope it can guide others as well!' Julie

At the end of the day, you got the position you have because you were deemed to be the best candidate for the role and you deserve to be in it. As such, you are valuable to the organisation. If you weren't, you wouldn't be in the role. Because you are valuable, you have something valuable to contribute to the meetings that you attend. This includes your thoughts, ideas and suggestions. Whilst your way of communicating your thoughts, ideas and suggestions may be different to how your extroverted colleagues do, just because there may be more of them doesn't mean that your contribution is not as equal as theirs. Accept that your style may be different to that of the extroverts in the room and accept that that is ok.

> '*As a Leader develops their Powers of Observation, I believe an associated confidence will accompany them. As their Knowledge and Experience increase, their observations become more powerful, and people around them have greater confidence in what they have to say. That builds trust in a team, and a more welcoming environment where everyone is more comfortable.*' John

As a leader, it is necessary to adapt leadership styles according to the situation in order to get the best possible outcome for the common good. This may require having to do things that do not play to your natural strengths, taking you out of your comfort zone. If your leadership team meetings are held in a way that doesn't play to your strengths, unless you are able to change things, or influence change, find ways to contribute in your own authentic way. The more you do it, the easier it will get, and the better at doing it you will become.

> '*I think that the tip to practise, practise, practise is very wise. An introvert can often appear as searching for words when speaking out on the spot at a meeting. An extroverted storyteller once advised me to treat the experience like acting where an actor ensures that he knows his lines before going on stage. He was correct that an introvert especially may need some pre-rehearsal and pre-self-scripting. I find that I need rehearsal time in order to come across as succinct and fluid with a polished delivery. The written rather than verbal method of communication is much more effortless for me.*' Aldean

It is often the case that meetings have been held the way they have for years and no one has ever questioned whether the way they are held is the most effective. Sometimes people go along with the way they are conducted and don't challenge the status quo for the sake of peace. If you are able to change or influence the way that meetings are conducted so they become more inclusive, then do so. Introduce meetings that are held in ways that play to both introverted and extroverted strengths. Just because your organisation has held meetings the way they are held since time immemorial doesn't mean that this is the best way to have them and it doesn't mean that they have to continue to be held this way.

Making sure that the agenda is sent out sufficient time in advance can make a big difference for those who are introverted. Typically, an agenda is set for the meeting and the intention is that during the meeting each item will be gone through in turn. Invariably, the agenda merely lists topics for discussion without giving any insight. If a short description as to the discussion around the agenda item can be given, and what is to be accomplished in the discussion, it means that people will be able to do some good preparation in advance. Many of the introverted women I work with tell me that productivity gets even more compromised if there is no meeting agenda, whereby a selected few will dominate the discussion. Or if the agenda is sent out too close to the meeting, there is insufficient time for it to be gone through and preparation for the meeting can't be done in advance.

'Over the years I've had many experiences of being in a room of people who love the sound of their own

voices, only to come out of the room completely confused and feeling like I'm an idiot because I'm missing their points and not speaking up enough. Sadly, there is pressure to speak up too often. Though when I do speak up, I tend to find those that speak more or louder are quite happy to cut me off. I'd rather be the person that listens, reflects and reacts accordingly and with something of true value.' Laura

In the article A Folk Theory of Meetings and Beyond, Ib Ravn presents his research showing that on a scale of 1 to 5, where 1 is very bad and 5 is very good, the response in which participants rated meetings was 3.3[7]. The article states that if a customer satisfaction survey showed such poor results, this would be big trouble for a private company. Yet meeting after meeting is held, and although thought of so poorly, they continue to be tolerated. Ravn proposes an alternative format of meeting, that of group facilitation. A facilitator (preferably someone neutral but this may not be possible) would make it easier for the group to accomplish its objectives. I believe that for the introverted, this way of conducting meetings will ensure that everyone is heard. By using different techniques, the facilitator can draw out what is needed from the group in a way that is inclusive.

'As a leader of these type of meetings, it is important to draw out everyone's thoughts rather than the extroverts controlling decision making and decisions. You may be missing valuable input and you also risk the problem of aligning the team when some are *holding back on input and silently don't support the direction.' Kathy*

The way that meetings are generally conducted with a chairperson, are very authoritarian, and arise from industrialisation, which had its emphasis on production. Meetings back then did not have a concern for the motivation of those attending. Facilitation, on the other hand, is conducted in a way that makes the meeting more meaningful to participants and therefore they are more likely to be motivated. I believe that this makes meetings more inclusive. Amazon CEO Jeff Bezos is reported to hold meetings that are more inclusive to the different personality types of people in the room[8]. People are given a topic or a memo that can be up to six pages and are asked to spend up to 30 minutes writing down their thoughts and then sharing them. These types of 'silent' meetings as they are known are being adapted by other organisations. I think holding meetings in this way is great for introverts because they give us time to think and give a carefully considered response.

'I find breaking into small groups for brainstorming during meetings leads to more involvement for all participants. It is less intimidating and more people contribute.' Mary

Another thing you could do is get each person to spend a few minutes writing down their thoughts on an issue, and then to pass their notes to the Chair or Facilitator. Responses can then be grouped together and read out, with a discussion and agreement reached. Similarly, go around the table giving each person a few minutes' uninterrupted time to share their thoughts and ideas around the topic to be discussed. That way everyone gets to say something of value and gets to be heard.

> 'Another suggestion is to urge the leader of the meeting to use various ways to get feedback from the audience. To prevent the same people from talking all the time, have everyone write down their suggestions in 3 minutes and then go around the room and have everyone read two items from their list. Or conduct a round-robin discussion. Everyone gets to talk for 1 minute and go around the entire room while the leader writes down feedback. If you are the leader and someone tries to dominate the room, cut them off, tell the person that they have some valuable feedback, but that you have to move on to keep the meeting on-track. (write down their suggestion) Follow up with another type of discussion if needed to get other input.' Jeri

We are all different for a reason. It would be a sad state of affairs if everybody was the same. When introverts and extroverts come together, they complement each other to give a grounded, whole thinking, balanced perspective on things. This can challenge thoughts and beliefs, allowing for collective creativity and innovative ideas and solutions.

If you are able to change the way meetings are conducted in your organisation (or if not, able to influence change at least), give consideration to some of the suggestions here.

'Introverts at meetings always reflect on everything and need time to evaluate their position. Speaking from experience, it is imperative to let the extroverts speak as that is indeed their most effective tool of communication. Introverts on the other hand will speak later and generally share information no one had time to evaluate when speaking before. Introverts are the quiet ones for sure, but that never means they don't have the right or better answer, they just wait until they believe they are at the right time to contribute. They never speak to be heard; they speak to share.' Jo

SELF-REFLECTION EXERCISE

- What is it about meetings that you don't like?
- What are your thoughts and beliefs about what will happen?
- If it was to happen, what could you do?
- What is a more helpful approach for you to have going forward?
- If those unhelpful thoughts and beliefs start to rear their head, what will you do to prevent yourself becoming fretful and anxious?
- What pre-meeting activities are you going to do?
- What will you do to ensure that you speak up?
- What will you do to ensure that you are listened to?

5 | *Thriving in an Extroverted Environment*

When my son was little, I used to feel tired regularly. Back then I didn't know about introversion/ extroversion, what drains our energy as introverts and how we need to recharge. I put my tiredness down to being a single mum, working full time and studying part time. Whilst that will have been a significant contributing factor, I now realise that it was partly due to the different energy levels of myself and my son. My son is an extrovert and he would be on the go from the minute he woke up in the morning until he went to sleep at night, wanting me to join in with him. I remember taking him to his after-school activities and popping home for a quick nap to recharge, before going to pick him up again. This chapter looks at how you can identify what drains your energy, what you can do about it, and how you can be at your best.

When I look back, I now realise why my son, with his extroverted energy, wanted us to be always talking, on the go and doing things, whereas I relished those moments of solitude when I could recharge and gather my thoughts. Back then, I never could understand why, when he was studying for his GCSEs and A Levels, he could have loud, upbeat music on and study at the same time.

The corporate environment here in the West is very much geared towards extroversion and the extroverted personality. It is often the case that she who shouts loudest and is the most gregarious is the one that gets ahead. Not only that, open plan offices (that we have seen a move towards over the years) don't provide an environment conducive to an introvert being able to thrive. Selection interviews, meetings, networking... many of the practices within organisations provide environments better suited to the extroverted energy. They are not the best environments in which introverts can thrive and be their best.

As an introvert working in such an environment, it can feel like you are under pressure to behave like your extroverted colleagues, and you may even try to act that way too. But doing so can be draining and can sap your energy, leaving you weary, stressed and lacking in confidence. When many of my clients come to me for coaching, they have been putting on a persona at work and acting in ways that are not them.

THERE'S ONLY SO LONG THAT YOU CAN PRETEND

Not long after taking on a role as an Associate Director, Annie told me she was faking it until she made it. This was draining her energy, and she feared that her colleagues could tell. Day after day, she felt continued pressure to be overly social with others at the company. Her boss is the epitome of an extrovert, which created even more pressure as she felt she had to emulate her behaviour. It didn't help that she worked in an open plan office and felt like others were watching her every move. Having been at the company for only two months, she decided to resume her search for a new work environment. She wondered, though, whether she was making the right move, or whether she would be letting the extroverts win.

When we try to be something that we're not, we can only keep the pretence up for so long before it starts to take its toll on us. By being your authentic, introverted self, you will fare much better in the long term. You will be more empowered, more motivated and have a natural confidence about you. If you find it challenging being your true introverted self in an extroverted environment, and you put on your pretentious extroverted mask every day to go to work, ask yourself: 'How does this really make me feel?' How does acting this way benefit you as an individual in the long term? There may be an unspoken expectation that extroverted behaviour is the norm in your organisation, but you don't have to go along with that norm. Remember, you CAN influence people's opinions about you.

Thriving in an extroverted environment means being able to be your best, authentic self without putting on an act, or constantly thinking you have to act in ways that go against who you are. It's about being at your optimum whilst knowing and understanding yourself, how you tick and how you can adapt to different situations without draining your energy. In order to thrive, self-acceptance, self-awareness and self-management are needed.

SELF-ACCEPTANCE

Have you accepted that you are introverted and that this is perfectly ok? Do you yourself hold misconceptions of introversion? Did you grow up being told that you were too quiet, that you needed to speak more, or were you made to feel that something was wrong with you because you were so quiet? Were you told as a child that you didn't raise your hand enough in class and speak up? If so, it's not surprising if you have introvert denial as an adult. After all, you've probably had a lifetime of other people making you believe that introversion is second class. Before you can lead others, you need to be able to lead yourself and if you want to help others to see the unfavourable biases they may hold against introverts, you need to start with yourself. You need to rid yourself of the negative unconscious bias that you yourself hold.

Have you accepted yourself as you are? Have you embraced your introverted nature? Loving and accepting yourself as you are means that you will no longer compare yourself to your extroverted colleagues and think you are not as good as them. You won't be concerned that you are not loud, gregarious or as popular as them. You will be accepting that you are quiet, and that you may be more reserved, but that is ok. Self-acceptance is covered in more detail in chapter 2, so if you have just jumped straight to this chapter, you might want to read chapter 2 before you carry on.

It can be liberating when we accept ourselves as the introverted women we are. We can take off the mask and be introvert and proud. For years I didn't accept myself as I was. I longed to be like the popular extroverts who got all the attention. The little, quiet me often felt invisible and like a nobody. When we look at others who appear to be more popular and outgoing than us and put ourselves down in the process, it can cause us to believe we are not good enough. But when we do that, we are looking at our situation through rose-tinted glasses. We are looking at an ideal that is not inclusive. Because of a lack of self-acceptance, some people have a desire for approval. Once we realise that we don't need approval from anyone else but ourselves, and actually believe it, we can look at our popular, extroverted friends and colleagues, be happy for them and not want to be like them.

For some of the introverted women I work with, they don't even have a desire to be popular and outgoing – the thought of it alone makes them cringe. The challenge for these women is that they've bought in to the lie that has been fed them over the years, so put themselves down, believing they are not good enough.

There are times when I look at how extroverts and introverts are treated differently and have previously thought that if I was extroverted, it would have been quicker for me to get ahead in my business because people tend to gravitate to those who are more outgoing and sociable. Even introverts may gravitate to extroverts in social situations because extroverts have a way of bringing out the side of an introvert that is not always seen.

I have learnt to not define myself, my life, or my view of what success means to me by way of a popular world view. I have learnt to look within at who I am and what matters to me, and to switch off from the noise and the distractions that would leave me insecure within myself, if I let them. What about you? Are you introvert and proud? Do you know who you are and what matters to you? Who defines who you should be or how you should live your life? Is it you, or have you bought in to an ideal of what others say you should be?

SELF-AWARENESS

Self-awareness is a key competency of emotional intelligence. Emotional self-awareness is the ability to understand your own emotions and how they impact your performance. Being self-aware, you pick up on other people's perception of you and are able to modify how you appear to others because you see the bigger picture[1]. When we are self-aware, we know what makes us tick. We know what turns us on and what turns us off. We know what energises us and what drains us. We know our strengths and limitations. We also know how we impact others and how others impact us. Self-awareness enables us to know when to modify or adapt our behaviour in order to achieve a desired outcome. It enables us to know when we need to take time out to energise and recharge.

We are often so busy on the treadmill of life that we aren't aware that we have control over how we feel, how we act and behave, and how we respond to situations. Many of us are operating on auto-pilot, our busy demanding lives not giving us the time to properly think and reflect. But making time to think and reflect about why you do certain things in a certain way, or why you respond to situations the way that you do, will help to increase your self-awareness. It will help you to see what you can do to respond differently if you need to.

Journaling is a great way of developing self-awareness. Self-reflecting by way of capturing your thoughts and emotions, writing them down, examining them and challenging them will help you get to know and understand who you really are. I have always had a good level of self-awareness, but it was doing the MSc Coaching Psychology and starting my coaching business that I started to make self-reflection a regular part of what I do. As a coach it is important that I have a reflective practice in order for me to grow and develop as a coach. It is just as important that I do this for my whole life and journaling is something that I do most days. By doing so I have become much more aware of who I am and why I respond to situations the way that I do. It has brought my unconscious biases into my consciousness and, I believe, made me a better person as a result.

Become aware of changes in bodily sensations as a result of different emotions that you experience. This could be your heart rate, breathing or tension in different parts of your body. Being aware of how your body responds to different emotions, environments and situations will enable you to identify what you can do to manage yourself and be at your optimal self.

FEEDBACK AND SELF-AWARENESS

As uncomfortable as it may be at times, getting feedback from others can help us to take an outside look at ourselves and to see ourselves through the lens of other people. To receive feedback, we have to be open to listening to what others have to say about us, even if we don't like what they say. As a leader you will have invariably had 360° feedback as part of your leadership development. Whilst 360° feedback has its pros and cons, use it as a guide to gauge the perception that other people have of you.

How do you respond to feedback? Do you go on the defensive if someone says something about you that you don't agree with? If so, examine your underlying thoughts and beliefs around why you do that. What causes you to respond the way that you do? If you don't have a 360° feedback system at work, you can always ask people to give you feedback of your own accord. Whether or not your workplace has a feedback system, get feedback from people who know you outside of work as well.

What can you learn from the feedback? What does it tell you about yourself? What does it tell you about how others perceive you? What can you learn about yourself from it?

SELF-MANAGEMENT

Self-awareness will enable you to identify how to apply self-management. Self-management is the ability to regulate your emotions and adapt your behaviour. It will enable you to take appropriate action when it comes to the environments that drain you. For example, if you know you have back-to-back meetings all day, you may find being in that particular environment draining. Because it is draining, you may find yourself withdrawing and going further into your own inner world during the meetings, and not actively engaging. In between meetings, go out and get some fresh air.

Likewise, if you are at a busy, full-on networking event that is full of buzz and white noise, you may find it irritating and draining. Step out of the room for a few minutes if you need to. At a networking drinks event after a busy day, it felt as if there was a loud buzz going on around me from so many people talking, that seemed to get louder and louder. I felt uncomfortable and, as a result, most definitely didn't want to engage in small talk with people that I didn't know. Because of my understanding and awareness that such environments were overly stimulating for me, I knew what was taking over.

I thought to myself that I would faint if I didn't get out, so I took myself out of the room to somewhere quiet for about 5 minutes to have a quick recharge, then went back in. The old me would not have understood why this was happening and would have thought that there was something wrong with me. This would have then made it even more difficult for me to engage with people, making for a very unpleasant experience. With that knowledge, I know the kind of networking environments that I am most likely to thrive in and those that it is best for me to avoid.

I don't particularly like those types of networking events that are just socials – a large group of people talking over drinks. And unless there is a real need for me to attend such an event, I try to avoid them. I prefer to attend networking events that have a focus. Ones where there is either a speaker, a panel discussion, or some other type of feature before an open networking session. That said, I love to go to parties, and in my younger days, nightclubs. I think the difference between that and a networking event that is just social is the music. I love to dance and listen to music. I would be quite content to go to a party and not have to engage in conversation, and just stay in my own world listening to the music and dancing all night. But, in order to be social (particularly if there are extroverts there), I modify my behaviour, adapt to the environment and make an effort to engage with others.

Research suggests that the work environment can affect a leader's wellbeing[2]. A poor fit between your work environment and your personality could have you feeling less engaged, less satisfied and less productive. Know when you need to step out of an environment to replenish your energy, rather than becoming completely drained. Another way in which you can give yourself a quick energy recharge is through breathing exercises. If you're feeling anxious or stressed, this calming breathing exercise is recommended by the National Health Service[3]. It takes just a few minutes and can be done anywhere:

You can do it standing up, sitting in a chair that supports your back, or lying on a bed or yoga mat on the floor. Make yourself as comfortable as you can. If you can, loosen any clothes that restrict your breathing. If you're lying down, place your arms a little bit away from your sides, with the palms up. Let your legs be straight, or bend your knees so your feet are flat on the floor. If you're sitting, place your arms on the chair arms. If you're sitting or standing, place both feet flat on the ground. Whatever position you're in, place your feet roughly hip-width apart.

- *Let your breath flow as deep down into your belly as is comfortable, without forcing it.*
- *Try breathing in through your nose and out through your mouth.*

- *Breathe in gently and regularly. Some people find it helpful to count steadily from 1 to 5. You may not be able to reach 5 at first.*
- *Then, without pausing or holding your breath, let it flow out gently, counting from 1 to 5 again if you find this helpful.*
- *Keep doing this for 3 to 5 minutes.*

If you are feeling drained of energy and need a quick recharge in the middle of your busy day, the following Bellows Breathing Technique (also known as The Stimulating Breath) will help to give you an energy boost[4]:

- *Sit in a comfortable upright position with your spine straight.*
- *With your mouth gently closed, breathe in and out of your nose as fast as possible. To give an idea of how this is done, think of someone using a bicycle pump (a bellows) to quickly pump up a tyre. The upstroke is inspiration and the downstroke is exhalation and both are equal in length.*
- *The rate of breathing is rapid with as many as 2-3 cycles of inspiration/expiration per second.*
- *While doing the exercise, you should feel effort at the base of the neck, chest and abdomen. The muscles in these areas will increase in strength the more this technique is practised. This is truly an exercise.*
- *Do this for no longer than 15 seconds when first starting. With practice, slowly increase the length of the exercise by 5 seconds each time. Do it as long as you are comfortably able, not exceeding one full minute.*
- *There is a risk of hyperventilation that can result in loss of consciousness if this exercise is done too much in the*

beginning. For this reason, it should be practised in a safe place such as a bed or chair.

This exercise can be used each morning upon awakening or when needed for an energy boost.

PLEASE NOTE: I am not a medical expert, nor am I a medical professional, so if you have any sort of breathing difficulties or conditions, I suggest you seek medical advice before carrying out these exercises.

As introverts we often have many thoughts racing around in our heads, and if the environment you are in is overly stimulating, it can create what I call that introvert buzz, otherwise known as overstimulation. Taking a mindfulness break, whereby you let your mind be still and do nothing for a couple of minutes, will also help you to recharge.

OPEN PLAN OFFICES

There has been a trend over the years to move to large open plan offices and hot desking but the open plan office is an introvert's nightmare. Designed to foster better teamwork, and save money, research actually shows that open plan offices are not the best working environment for both introverts AND extroverts. In a study where employees switched from individual cubicles to open plan offices, it was found that they spent 73% less time in face-to-face interactions, 67% more time on email and 75% more time on instant messenger[5].

Cindy very much struggled with open plan offices, something that became even more so over time. She found it really hard to focus. She found it hugely distracting. It drained her and sapped her energy levels. If she was particularly tired, she actually found working in an open plan environment overwhelming and distressing. Her dislike of open plan offices was a huge contributing factor in her bid to 'escape' the corporate world and ultimately work/thrive in an environment more suited to her introverted personality.

If you work in an open plan office, sit by the window if possible. Being near to the window and daylight will feel less closed in. Failing that, sit near to the door. Make sure you take your lunch break and go outside for a walk. If you are able to, work from home as often as you can, to avoid the environment as much as possible. If that is not possible, start your day earlier so that you are there before the majority of people arrive so you don't have to spend as much time in the buzzy environment.

If there is a poor fit between your personality and the environment you work in, what can you do to manage yourself and the environment?

INCREASE AWARENESS ABOUT WHAT INTROVERSION IS AND IS NOT

Help to change the narrative by increasing awareness about what introversion is and is not. Your extroverted colleagues may have bought in to the misconceptions so help them to see that being an introvert doesn't make you any less than your louder, extroverted colleagues. Help them to see the benefits that introverts bring to the table. Show them that loud and fast isn't always the best and that reflection and having time to think are also needed to make accurate, informed decisions.

Let them know that just because you don't always join in the banter, it doesn't mean that you are being rude, or that you are ignorant or stuck up. It means that you don't always want to make small talk and prefer to talk about things that are more meaningful to you. Let them know that you like to have moments of solitude, rather than always being socially connected, because that's how you recharge and perform at your best.

UNDERSTAND WHAT MAKES YOUR EXTROVERTED COLLEAGUES TICK

At the same time, have an appreciation for what makes your extroverted colleagues tick. After all, you have to work together and get along with them, so there does need to be some give and take. Even though you may feel like you're the one that is constantly giving by trying to be something that you're not, you still need to find a way to engage with them. If the topics that they talk about don't interest you, start conversations that you can engage in.

It's not about you faking it and pretending to be something that you're not. It's about you being your authentic introverted self, whilst at the same time recognising that your extroverted colleagues also need to be their authentic extroverted selves.

BE INTROVERT AND PROUD

With the self-assurance that you are introvert and proud, you can then confidently help others to see the unfavourable unconscious bias they have towards introverts. You won't need to worry about not being accepted, because you will realise that you don't need the acceptance or approval of others, and that you are good enough as you are. As an introvert, trying to act like the extroverts by being something that you're not will only make you weary and exhausted. Be yourself. Be introvert and proud, and thrive rather than it feel like it's a drain to survive.

As a leader who is introverted, you may find that your role can drain your energy because of the need to act in more extroverted ways at times. Without an understanding of the difference between how introverts and extroverts are stimulated, this may even cause you to think that there is something wrong with you. In her PhD dissertation titled A Method To My Quietness: A Grounded Theory Study Of Living and Leading With Introversion, Dr Leatrice Oram found that three theoretical propositions emerged from her studies, namely[6]:

- *Enacting leadership has significant costs for an introverted leader's energy and identity*
- *An introverted leader must adopt a conscious learning orientation to leadership development, including experimentation with possible leader identities*

- *Effective introverted leadership is dependent on understanding the powerful intersectionality of introversion, relationship, and identity*

Thriving as an introvert in an extroverted environment is about being able to be your best self in all situations. It requires you to identify situations where you are at your optimum and situations where you are not. Where you are not, it requires you to look at what you can do to be your best possible self in those environments. Working through your thoughts and emotions and being able to manage them is a key factor to being able to thrive. The preferred way for working through emotions and information for many of the participants in Dr Oram's study was internally (something I myself and my clients prefer to do). This enabled them to get ready for interacting with other people. It also enabled them to absorb information.

Building thinking and reflecting time into your week will help you to better your thinking process. It will also help to increase your self-awareness and identify when the environment is draining your energy. My client Emily was feeling stressed by the environment that she worked in, and as a result it affected her perception about herself and her role as a director. During coaching, one of the things she identified that she would do differently was to set time in her diary for thinking and reflecting. She treated this like she would any other meeting, putting her out of office reply on, and setting her phone to voicemail so she wouldn't be disturbed.

I don't think that it is just senior leaders that should make time to think and reflect. I think people at all levels could benefit from having space in their working day for reflection from time to time. I believe that it would enhance performance and help make for a more productive and happier workforce. Many people get so caught up in the busyness of their working days that they don't stop to reflect on what they're thinking about. Be mindful, though, that you don't overthink and go into deep rumination, as this is one of the downsides of reflecting. If this happens, it can narrow perspective, cause inaction, and even lead to anxiety if you allow it to. This was something that some of the participants in Dr Oram's study identified with. Reflect, but don't go into a deep rumination.

In her book *The Introvert Advantage: How to Thrive in an Extroverted World*, Dr Marti Olsen Laney talks about the energy crisis that introverts can have[7]. When your energy reserves are low, you need to make sure you're giving yourself enough downtime. According to Dr Laney, some of the symptoms that you may experience are trouble sleeping or eating; frequent colds; headaches; back pain; or allergies. She says you may also feel anxious, be agitated, be irritable, be snappy, unable to think or concentrate or make decisions, be confused, feel drained, and more... She calls these 'red flags' and they are warning you that you are having an energy crisis. In order to be at our optimal best, we need to ensure that our energy levels are not depleted and that we don't get into an energy crisis. That is why self-awareness is so important, so that you can easily identify when you are tipping over into an energy crisis. I find that I am more easily distracted when my energy levels are low, and I can end up procrastinating and self-sabotaging as a result.

Be sure to schedule downtime in your diary on a regular basis, particularly if you are often in environments that overstimulate and drain your energy. As I have developed my self-awareness over the years, I have come to realise what the triggers are for depleting my energy and as a result I am able to put things in place to remedy this. As you develop your self-awareness, you will start to recognise those meetings which drain your energy the most, or which types of social events leave you drained. With this awareness, you can find ways of making sure that you have those little recharge breaks that you need. Whether it is building time around the event, or slipping in a quick recharge by going for a walk in the fresh air, it is important that at the end of a long busy day you give yourself downtime.

For some of you, your life may feel as if you are on a treadmill and running at a fast pace and there is no stop button. But it is important that you have downtime when you can recollect your thoughts and reflect uninterrupted, working through your thoughts and feelings. This is particularly important if you are surrounded by people all day and you don't have your own space or time on your own.

Part of being able to thrive in an extroverted environment means you will need to step out of your comfort zone at times, if you are to engage and to get on. As a leader, certain situations will call for you to behave in ways which are more typical of those who are extroverted. You will need to be able to adapt to different situations and adjust your style accordingly. I cover adapting in chapter 8, but for now, when you are in situations where you need to adapt your style to a more 'extroverted' way of being, do what needs to be done in order to get the results needed, but manage yourself and your energy. The longer you adapt for, the more of a drain it will be on your energy. Take the necessary breaks that you require. Develop your inner confidence so that you are able to step out of your comfort zone when necessary and deal with those situations.

To me, confidence means being comfortable with who I am and having the courage to do all that I need to do. As such, there may be occasions when I feel a bit fearful about doing something, or maybe even lacking the confidence to do it because it might be something I've never done before. But because I know who I am and I am comfortable with who I am, that is not a barrier to me doing what I need to do. I will develop the courage to do it even though I may be feeling fearful, and then the more I do something the more confident at it I become.

I see this regularly with clients who say they lack confidence because they are not experienced in something, or because of their perceptions of how they view it. Once they change the way that they think about what it is that they need to do, and the way that they view it, they are naturally more confident. When they go ahead and do it again and again and again, that gives them a new level of confidence.

It can be easy to stay stuck in a comfort zone and as a result not get the opportunities that you want. Tina wanted to take her leadership career to the next level and go for Director level roles. She was very much aware of her strengths and utilised them in her work. But what she did was do the things which were in her comfort zone and that she was familiar with. This is what had been holding her back. Rather than stretching herself to utilise her strengths in ways which would enable her to demonstrate her abilities at that more senior level, she was playing it safe by staying in her comfort zone. I challenged her to step out of her comfort zone and pitch herself at the level she aspired to. She started attending higher level meetings and taking the lead on projects on behalf of her manager where she was able to network and develop relationships with those more senior in the organisation, as well as stakeholders of a more senior level.

Stepping out of your comfort zone and putting yourself in more challenging situations and environments may seem daunting. When stepping out of your comfort zone, stretch yourself so that it feels slightly uncomfortable, but don't go too far as you will end up in a stress zone. The more you stretch yourself and do different things in this way, the more confident you will become at it. But remember, the more time you spend adapting, the more energy you will use up, so be sure to build in sufficient downtime to recharge.

SELF-REFLECTION EXERCISE

- What environments and situations do you least thrive in?
- What can you do to be at your best in those environments and situations, whilst getting the outcome that is required?
- How will you manage your energy levels?
- What will you do to recharge?
- What can you do to raise awareness of what introversion is and is not, and the unfavourable bias that exists?

6 | *Positioning*

When I got my last leadership promotion as an employee, it was as a result of strategically positioning myself two years previously. Whilst networking at a leadership conference, I became aware that a temporary senior role would be coming up the following year in another area of the organisation – a role that I wanted to apply for. When a position at the level I was currently at then came up in that area shortly after the conference, I applied for it and made a sideways move. That was part of me strategically positioning myself for the more senior role. The reason why I did this was so that I could raise my visibility in that area, and come under the radar of those who would be making the decision about filling the role I was ultimately interested in. Once in the role, I took on additional responsibilities, led on area wide projects, and deputised for my manager. When the position I was interested in was advertised, I applied for it and I got it. Whether you want to go for promotion, make a career transition, establish credibility, or even exit the corporate world to start your own business, give some thought to what you can do to position yourself to achieve it.

As someone who coaches introverted women leaders, and as an introvert who climbed the leadership ladder myself, I am aware of the challenges faced with regard to promoting yourself and raising your visibility in order to get ahead. Many of the self-promotion activities typically associated with positioning yourself for opportunities may not appeal to you. However, there are ways that you can do it that feel more authentic. This chapter shows you some of these ways.

DEVELOP A VISION AND A PLAN

Having a vision for your career and a plan will be the road map that helps you to focus on what it is you need to do in order to achieve your career goals. It is easier to pick yourself up from setbacks or overcome obstacles if you know the direction in which you want to go. An exercise I often do in my career development workshops to help participants create a vision for their career and to develop their career plan, is to get them to fast forward in their minds to their 80th birthday. They are going to have a party with family and friends attending from all over the world and will be presented with a lifetime achievement award. They will give a speech about their achievements over the years. Questions to help them reflect and prepare their speech are:

- What and/or whom did I impact?
- Whom did I care for? How did I impact or change this person/people?
- What were my major achievements at the age of 20, 30, 40, 50, 60 and 70?
- What did I show interest in? What was I passionate/enthusiastic about?
- What character traits and values did I consistently demonstrate over my lifetime?
- Reflecting on my responses to the above questions, how will this shape my vision for my life and career?

Why don't you do the exercise and use it to shape your vision for your life and career, then plan out what the steps are you will need to take in order to achieve it? Once created, your plan is not set in stone and can be adapted to accommodate changes along the way.

LET OTHERS BLOW YOUR HORN AND GET A SPONSOR

Navigating the path to the executive suite is not an easy one for many women, both introvert and extrovert. With barriers and hurdles to overcome, having someone as your cheerleader, who champions your cause, helps to make the journey less fraught. That is where a sponsor comes in. A sponsor is a person of influence who becomes an advocate for someone who is looking to progress in their career. They use their influence with decision makers to recommend aspiring, high potential individuals, and open doors of opportunity for them. Because of the typically quiet nature of introverts, those decision makers who need to know about your successes and achievements may not be aware of you as much as they are of your more vocal, extroverted colleagues. Sponsorship goes beyond mentoring, and sponsors are able to open doors to opportunities that you may not otherwise have had access to[1].

There is a saying that goes 'self-praise is no recommendation', and what could be better than having a person of influence recommend you as being the ideal person for a role? In environments where there is lots of 'noise' by way of people self-promoting, in order to stand out, having someone who will do the promoting for you is like having Idris Elba (*substitute Idris for whoever you want!*) spot only you in a crowded arena.

The recruitment and selection process has its biases when it comes to introverts too. Having someone who knows you and your work well, and can promote you to the powers that be, can help dispel the myths about introversion to those who are making selection decisions. Through their influential networks, a sponsor will be more aware of opportunities that arise before you are. If reports that between 60-80% of jobs are not advertised (known as the hidden job market) but filled through referrals and by way of networking are to be believed, having a sponsor can only be a good thing, particularly if you don't like networking. A sponsor can make you aware of those opportunities as and when they arise and could be your key to opening the door to the hidden job market.

If there are so many jobs that are filled through networking or referral, this means people are making introductions and recommendations through their networks to fill these roles. Because of their position of influence, a sponsor is able to use this influence and recommend you. Studies show that women do not utilise their networks as effectively as men[2]. This is both due to women often being excluded from powerful networks, as well as to internal barriers that women have concerning networking. Having a sponsor can open the door to influential networks, giving you access to opportunities you may otherwise never even get to hear of.

A sponsor will actively support you in your career advancement and can help accelerate your career more quickly than you can do on your own. Having one can benefit your career by 22-30%[3]. Not only will they recommend you, and connect you to senior decision makers, they will promote you and open doors of opportunities for you. Because a sponsor will blow your trumpet and recommend you to valuable contacts you would otherwise not have access to, it will enable you to speed up your career progression.

If you want to get promoted, when thinking about who you want to be your sponsor, don't just look within your organisation. Also think about influential stakeholders who can blow your trumpet for you. Gloria was very respected and admired for her work by stakeholders but was not well known to the CEO. In one of our coaching sessions I helped her to see the benefits of sponsors, and in particular with her situation, stakeholders as sponsors. One particular major stakeholder who had a good relationship with the CEO would promote Gloria to the CEO and tell him about the great work Gloria was doing with their organisation, and how brilliant she was at it. The CEO was impressed by the impact Gloria was having on stakeholders and started to take a keen interest in her work. When a position that Gloria wanted became available, the seed had already been sown and she got the promotion.

Even if you have a sponsor, you still need to put in the work and get the position on your own merit. Think of it as similar to when you want some work doing at home and you ask friends for recommendations of tried and trusted tradesmen they have used. They may recommend someone they think is brilliant, but that person will still have to prove themselves to you before you hire them to do the work. That is how it works with sponsorship. A sponsor will give you access to opportunities and recommend you, but at the end of the day, it will be down to you to prove that you are the best person for the role.

NETWORK THE INTROVERTED WAY

The benefits of networking for career advancement have been well documented for many years, and having a diverse network is beneficial for career success. There is a lot to be said for the old saying 'it's not what you know, but who you know'. However, for many introverted women, networking is something they do not enjoy. Whether you are looking for an internal promotion, looking to go elsewhere, or looking to achieve your business aspirations, include networking as part of your positioning strategy. The challenge with networking for many introverts is that the environment of many networking events can be overstimulating. Noisy, packed rooms full of small talk are not necessarily the ideal way we introverts want to spend our time. Spending too long in such environments can be energy draining for us. If you are an introvert who doesn't like networking, it CAN become an enjoyable experience, and you CAN do it in a way that works for you.

DON'T VIEW NETWORKING
AS A DIRTY WORD

What thoughts do you conjure up in your mind when you think about networking? Do you think noisy crowds and small talk, the thought of which drains your energy? Or do you view it as an opportunity to connect with people and develop relationships? I don't know about you, but as an introvert myself, thinking about networking as a way of connecting and developing meaningful relationships feels so much better than viewing it as a loud, noisy 'meat market', full of small talk.

It hasn't always been like that for me. I have had to learn how to network in ways that work for me. When I first started my business and was complaining that my business wasn't getting off the ground, working with a coach, I realised that I was procrastinating about networking. I didn't like the thought of having to go and 'work a room', making small talk with lots of different people that I didn't know. Making valuable connections is what networking is about. It's an opportunity to connect with people and develop and nurture relationships. And these relationships may lead to opportunities, or they may lead to mutually beneficial arrangements. Change the way you think about networking and you will change the way you feel about it. That is what worked for me and the introverted women I have coached about networking.

In some networking environments, the conversations can be shallow, with people making small talk that comes across as self-centred as people try to sell themselves or their services. For the introverted woman, this can be off-putting. I remember once when I was at a networking event speaking to someone, a woman marched up to us, thrust her business card in our hands and proceeded to give us a running commentary about who she was and what she did before sauntering off to find her next victim. She didn't show any interest in finding out who we were and what we did. Those who come across as self-centred, making the conversation all about them and what they have to offer, probably don't understand how to get the best out of networking, or may possibly be new to it. Or they may just be downright self-centred!

If you prefer deep and meaningful conversations to small talk, view the small talk as a segue to a more deep and meaningful conversation. Rather than thinking you have to work the room and make small talk with lots of different people, have conversations with fewer people that are deeper and more meaningful, the small talk being the ice breaker to get there. Go for quality conversations rather than quantity. Bear in mind that many extroverts are stimulated by the social interaction of busy networking events and as such enjoy talking to lots of people, so don't be put off if you're having an interesting conversation with someone who is extroverted and they race off to go and start a conversation with someone else.

If you're not sure what to talk about, ask open questions – questions that begin with what, where, when, who or how. Once you get past the initial 'what do you do?' etc, to keep the conversation flowing, if there has been a guest speaker at the event, you could pick up on a particular point from the talk. For example, you could ask, 'What did you think about what xxxxx said about xxxx in their talk?' Or you could ask what it was about the event that appealed to them. By asking open questions, it means the other person has to respond with more than a yes or no answer. This will enable you to pick up on what they say and ask other open questions based on their response. Doing this will help to get the conversation flowing.

I often find that the reason many introverted women don't like networking is not because they lack confidence, but because they are not playing to their strengths. Being surrounded by extroverts can make them believe that there is something wrong with them. They find it challenging to work the room and flit from conversation to conversation, and don't realise that extroverts are stimulated in this way. They may try to do the same thing but feel more and more awkward and it drains their energy as they go about it. It's a bit like the quote "Everybody is a genius. But if you judge a fish by its ability to climb a tree, it will live its whole life believing that it is stupid." As an introvert, if you're going to try and do what the extroverts do, that's what it will feel like: being a fish out of water. Play to your strengths and be yourself. People love to feel that they are being listened to and introverts generally prefer to listen and reflect, so use this to your advantage. Remember, though, that you will have to do some talking, but develop conversations in a way that comes naturally to you.

Just as you may feel uncomfortable, there are bound to be others there who feel uncomfortable too. Keep your eyes out for other people in the room who feel awkward about networking and start conversations with them. They will probably welcome your friendly face approaching them. It is often easy to spot someone who feels uncomfortable at a networking event; they may be standing on their own, or have a general look of awkwardness about them. Use the open question approach to break the ice and enter into a deep, meaningful conversation with them.

Because networking may be overstimulating for you, allow yourself sufficient time after the event to recharge and rejuvenate. Spending a long time in such environments can be mentally exhausting, so plan ahead if you know you have such events coming up. You may also find that you need to recharge during the course of the event, in which case take yourself outside and get some fresh air.

Business development and bringing in new clients was a requirement of Alison as a solicitor, but she hated networking. Going to networking events with the sole purpose of drumming up new clients felt clinical and cold to her. By helping her to reframe her thoughts and beliefs about networking, she changed her perspective about it. Rather than viewing it as being a marketplace where everyone was trying to sell their wares, she came to view it as an opportunity to meet new people and start to build relationships. She could then develop and nurture those relationships away from the networking environment and introduce those who needed it to the benefits of what her organisation could do for them. She also made sure she allowed herself sufficient time to recharge her energy levels after attending networking events.

This change in perspective made networking more tenable for her and whilst it never became her most favourite activity, she started to enjoy it. This along with having fewer but more deep and meaningful conversations (as opposed to putting pressure on herself by trying to work the room like a social butterfly) made networking a more pleasurable experience.

NETWORK ON LINKEDIN

Whilst not just for introverts, reconnecting with your contacts on LinkedIn and meeting for a coffee (this can be face to face or virtual is a great way to identify opportunities if you are looking to go elsewhere. You can find out about the culture of organisations you are interested in too by connecting with people who work there and finding out more about the organisations. Don't just take, though. Give something as well, and offer to help your connections in some way.

Angela, who hadn't previously used LinkedIn much and didn't enjoy networking, wanted to go for an executive role. I encouraged her to start using LinkedIn as part of her positioning strategy and to reconnect with her connections. It turned out that one connection she contacted was a non-executive director on the board of an organisation she had applied to. Because of their knowledge of her and her experience, this director was able to vouch for her credibility with colleagues. At the interview she demonstrated that she was the best person for the role, and she got the job. Whilst she got the role on her own merit, it will have helped that her connection was able to validate her credibility.

MAKE YOUR ACHIEVEMENTS KNOWN TO THOSE WHO NEED TO KNOW

Often not being ones for self-promotion it means that introverts can sometimes get overlooked or side stepped. Preferring to let your work speak for itself means you run the risk of not being heard by those who need to know. I would often get told by my manager that I needed to speak up more about my achievements. Not being one to brag or boast, I preferred to let my work speak for itself. That is, until I found ways of promoting myself and my achievements in ways that worked for me.

Whether it is at a networking event, a promotional interview, or going for a new job, talk about the results you have achieved with those who need to know. Rather than making it all about 'me, me, me', focus on the benefits to the organisation, the difference made and the role that you played in it. Whilst it is important to acknowledge the part the team played in getting results, introverts often make it ALL about the we, downplaying their role. Drop putting too much focus on the 'we' and demonstrate the value that you as an individual added. Acknowledge and praise your team, but at the same time remember that too much focus on the 'we' can come across like the part you played was insignificant. Don't wait for your annual performance review to inform your manager of your accomplishments. Keep them updated on a regular basis. That way, when it comes to you applying for promotion, your accomplishments have been well documented in your manager's mind.

Who else needs to know about your achievements? Who is it that you want to influence with your work? What can you do to make them aware of you? Identify who this is and how you can make them aware of who you are and what makes you so good at what you do. This could be by talking to them directly, including them in emails where appropriate, or even through stakeholders and other people who are influential to them. Make sure that they are aware of your successes and achievements, again focusing on the results and the difference that this has made, not making it self-centred, but about the value that you added.

DO THE WORK ON YOU

Identify what is required for the role you aspire to and do any developmental work on yourself that is needed. Get feedback to see whether others perceive you as a leader at that level and identify what you can do differently if they don't. Use your skills of listening and reflection to identify organisational problems, and come up with creative and innovative solutions that demonstrate your ability to think beyond your current role.

Let it be known to the powers that be that you are keen to go for more senior roles. Talk to people who are at the level that you aspire to and find out what it is like for them. Do some job shadowing to see what it is like practically. Volunteer to cover for your manager in their absence. Seek out developmental opportunities and responsibilities that demonstrate what you are capable of, and when that promotional opportunity arises, go for it.

As an introverted leader, you don't have to make a lot of noise and shout about how fabulous you are in order to be visible and stand out. You can be quietly visible and stand out in a way that plays to your strengths and feels more natural to you.

LET YOUR PASSION SHINE THROUGH

Have you ever observed someone when they are talking about something that they are passionate about? What is it that you notice? When we are passionate about what we do, it is hard to hide it from others. Just talking about something we are passionate about makes our faces light up. It gives off an air of self-assuredness and people are inspired by what we have to say. To have passion for what you do, your work needs to be important to you, aligning with your core values and being intrinsically motivating. If you are currently in a job that you hate and are therefore not passionate about it, putting aside the actual job, think about your strengths, your skills and the nature of the work you do enjoy doing. People are drawn to passionate people and by letting your passion for what you do shine through, people are more likely to take note and listen.

DEMONSTRATE THOUGHT LEADERSHIP THROUGH WRITING

Whether it is writing articles, blogging, making advice videos, doing talks, or answering questions in groups and forums, showcase your credibility and knowledge about your subject area through a medium that is most suited to you. Write or talk about what you know. Offer advice, offer solutions, demonstrate thought leadership. Become known as an authority for what it is that you do within your circle of influence. You don't need to call yourself a thought leader, but this will be what people see you as. Doing this allows you to promote yourself by showcasing your expertise without making it feel like it's 'me, me, me'.

Write articles and blogs that showcase your knowledge and expertise. Offer solutions to issues faced in your profession, or ideas that demonstrate your innovation. Writing is a great way to raise your profile and demonstrate thought leadership. You could start your own blog, write articles for your company's intranet site, contribute to industry specific publications, or publish articles on LinkedIn or other online publishing platforms.

SOCIAL MEDIA

Sharing your knowledge and expertise is so easy to do by way of videos these days. Use your smartphone and do short video clips, then upload to LinkedIn or whichever platform you want to raise your profile on. Or set up a YouTube channel and share the videos to the social media platforms of your choice. Some suggestions are sharing tips, offering your perspective on what is going on in your industry. Explaining new legislation/regulations that affects your industry in layman's terms and how it affects people, or sharing information about what people need to be aware of for key dates in your industry's calendar year, etc. You could even do a Q&A session via live stream.

If there are topical items in the news about your area of expertise, find articles and comment on them and share them. Keep abreast of what is going on within your industry, and as changes happen, talk about them on social media. Share content written by influencers in your field, adding your perspective before you post it. Comment on their posts and join in the discussions. Ask them questions about what they have shared and engage in conversation with them. Join online groups that are related to your profession and answer questions that people ask. Share your knowledge and your points of view. Talk about your achievements, focusing on the results and the difference made because of the action you took. 'Listen' to discussions and challenges that people talk about on social media that are within your subject area, and through your responses, demonstrate to people that you know your stuff.

Do work that is of a standard that other people want to sing your praises about, and whilst they are singing them, ask them to put the praise in a LinkedIn recommendation. Social media is here to stay, and many opportunities come about through social media. If you are an introverted leader who is not utilising social media as part of your career or leadership positioning strategy, you could be missing out.

CHANGE THE WAY YOU THINK ABOUT SELF-PROMOTION

The word self-promotion can conjure up feelings of being self-centred and can feel like it is bragging and boasting. That in itself can cause you to run away from doing it. What is it that you want to gain through self-promotion? Is it a promotion? Is it a new job? Is it recognition for all your hard work? Whatever it is that you want to gain through self-promotion, focus on that, and on how letting the relevant people know about your achievements is the vehicle to help you achieve that objective. Rather than allowing self-promotion to make you feel uncomfortable because it doesn't feel natural, changing your thoughts and beliefs about it will help to change how you feel about it.

BE YOURSELF

Just because other people may be making a lot of noise and shouting out 'look at me and how fabulous I am' doesn't mean you have to try and be the same. If you do, not only will it feel uncomfortable, but it could come across as inauthentic. If you want to get ahead in your field and get the recognition you deserve, if people don't know you or what it is your achievements are, making yourself visible will bring you under the radar of those who need to know. Be yourself, play to your natural strengths, and when you need to promote yourself, do it in a way that is authentic to you. There is a difference between showcasing your expertise, your knowledge and achievements, and bragging and boasting. Not one for giving a running commentary of my every movement online, I have learnt to network online and promote myself in ways that feel right for me. This has mainly been done through my writing and has resulted in me being named a LinkedIn Top Voice UK for three years running.

There will be times when you need to bring attention to what you have achieved, if you want to get ahead as a leader. Whether it is promoting yourself internally within your existing organisation, or externally to come under the radar of those you want to influence, there are many benefits to self-promotion that will help you achieve this. And remember, self-promotion doesn't have to feel uncomfortable, or as if you are bragging and boasting, if it is done in a way that works for you.

SELF-REFLECTION EXERCISE

- What is your area of expertise and what do you want to be known for?
- Who needs to know about you and what you do?
- What can you do to position yourself for your next move (whether upwards, sideways or something totally different altogether)?
- What will you put in place to make it happen?

7 | *Quiet Presence*

They say never judge a book by its cover, yet first impressions count. How many times have you made a snap judgement about someone based on what you see in those initial moments that you encounter them? I am sure that when you first meet a person, you are summing them up in some way. As a leader, having a good presence can be the difference between creating a movement and bringing everybody along, and everyone abandoning ship. If you aspire to be influential and impactful as a leader, you need to give some consideration to your presence.

'Executive presence' is a term we have increasingly heard of over recent years. Whilst there is no definitive guide to presence, there are some research-based suggestions as to what it is. Susan Bates of Bates Communications (who designed the first research-based scientifically validated assessment tool to measure executive presence and influence) states, 'To stand out and drive an organisation forward, you must own the room, project an authentic and confident style, excite people's imaginations and win hearts and minds.'[1] She states that executive presence is a must if you are to become influential and lead large-scale, complex business initiatives.

Through their research, Bates Communications identified three dimensions to executive presence, namely:

- Style
- Substance
- Character

Within each of these three dimensions are up to 15 facets that, when brought together, create an aura of presence that helps a leader make impact. Style is about what is observable about you based on the image you portray, your interpersonal behaviour, and the way that you behave. Substance includes the way you conduct yourself, how you act socially, and gravitas. Character comprises the personal traits, values and beliefs that make up who you are.

Research by the Centre for Talent Innovation identified three pillars to executive presence[2], namely:

- Gravitas (how you act)
- Communication (how you speak)
- Appearance (how you look)

Gravitas is the core characteristic with six identified behaviours of exuding confidence, acting decisively, showing integrity, demonstrating emotional intelligence, burnishing reputation and projecting vision. Communication includes great speaking skills, ability to command a room and ability to read an audience. Appearance acts mainly as a filter through which your communication skills and gravitas become more apparent, and includes good grooming and physical attributes.

Whilst there are a number of other views on what executive presence is, they all basically boil down to a similar thing. That is, the way you show up, the way you are perceived, and the impact you make.

Most people know presence when they see it in someone. I think a good contrasting example of leaders doing the same role who had it and who didn't can be seen in former Prime Ministers Tony Blair and Gordon Brown. Putting aside political persuasions, to me Tony Blair had presence as Prime Minister, whereas Gordon Brown did not. What world leaders (both men and women) do you think have the 'wow' factor? What is it about them that you see that qualifies them? When it comes to women, for me Michelle Obama, Sheryl Sandberg, Oprah Winfrey and Arianna Huffington come to mind. From their poise to their ability to command a room, I would say that these women have got presence.

Judith Denton is a social entrepreneur, singer and songwriter, and she has presence. I met her at the end of a 2018 International Women's Day event. As the group of women I was with were leaving the venue, she was also leaving, having been at another event in the same building. Just her appearance alone screamed presence. And that was before she had even opened her mouth. When we did get to speak to her, that presence was further validated by the way she spoke and what she spoke about. Had she been dressed differently, and not looked so striking, she may well have been missed by us. What does your appearance say about you?

For the purpose of this book, I am going to focus on the areas that introverted women tell me they find most challenging. These are exuding confidence, commanding the room, and acting decisively.

EXUDING CONFIDENCE

No matter how you feel on the inside, people will only see on the outside what you let them see. If you are lacking confidence, it doesn't mean that you have to let that show on the outside. If you want to be a serious contender for the boardroom, or your first leadership role, if you come across like you lack confidence, it will not instil trust.

Having the courage to stand up and speak out is necessary if you are to have presence. Courage is not the absence of fear, but the ability to do what is needed despite feeling fearful. Think back to chapter 2 where I mentioned the effect our emotions can have on our behaviour, which is as a result of what we think and believe about ourselves and our situations. Pinpoint those situations where you lack confidence and pinpoint exactly what it is that you lack confidence in, rather than giving yourself a blanket 'I lack confidence'.

We all lack confidence at something at some point or another in our lives, so rather than giving yourself a general all over-rating of lacking confidence, which is inaccurate, pinpoint exactly what it is that you lack confidence in. Is it standing up and speaking before a group of people? Is it having to make on-the-spot decisions? Is it that you don't plan properly, or need to develop your skills? Whatever it is that causes you to not be able to exude confidence, pinpointing exactly what it is makes it easier for you to address.

To exude confidence means having an air of self-assuredness about who you are and what you do. Be knowledgeable about your role, your subject area, and the topics that you need to address. When we are uncertain about what we are doing, it can cause our confidence to wane. Whether it's a meeting, a presentation you need to deliver, or walking into a room of influencers, planning and preparation is key. I often see women going into situations where they need to have presence, and a lack of planning and preparation has been their downfall. A lack of adequate preparation means they have to think on their feet – something they are not comfortable doing, and something that doesn't play to their strengths.

YOUR MINDSET

If you are able to address your mindset when it comes to exuding confidence, the other things will fall into place more easily. Picture two scenarios. In the first one think of something you need to do that you are not feeling confident about and in which you believe that you will not come across as confident. Something that you are feeling anxious over and worrying about. If you don't have anything coming up soon, use the scenario of having to do a presentation before the Board to persuade them to invest in your idea. You are feeling anxious, feeling nervous, and you've been worrying about it for weeks. Feeling like that, how do you think you will perform?

In the second scenario, the situation is the same as in scenario one. However, this time you are going to examine your thoughts and beliefs about what it is that you need to do. What could your thoughts and beliefs be that are causing you to feel so anxious, nervous and worried? Once you've identified them, challenge those thoughts and beliefs. What is a more rational way of looking at the situation? What is a more helpful way? If the worst was to happen, what could you do? Not only that, if your best friend came to you with the same issue, what would you tell her to do? Now take that advice and apply it to yourself.

How do you feel about it now? If you were to go into the situation feeling like you do now, how do you think you would perform?

BODY LANGUAGE

Effective communication is a key requirement for good leaders, and it is not just your written or verbal communication that is important. The silent communication, i.e. non-verbal communication, is of equal (if not greater) importance. Our body language has a significant impact on how we communicate and how our message is received and understood, and the perception others have of our leadership effectiveness. It can make us exude confidence, or it can make us appear timid. It can help people warm to us, or it can turn people off us.

The influence you have as a leader depends on how you are perceived by those you lead. Your body language and non-verbal communication are part of the mix that shapes the perception that others have of you, often without them even realising it.

One study found that leaders who used positive hand gestures created more immediacy between them and their followers and were considered to be more attractive than those who used negative hand gestures or no gestures at all[3]. Leaders who used no hand gestures or negative gestures were perceived to be distant. Another study found that leaders who used animated facial expressions, dynamic hand and body gestures, showed vocal fluency, and maintained eye contact, were perceived as charismatic, more so than when they did not[4].

SELF-MONITORING

Because we introverts tend to be less expressive and more reserved[5], knowing the link between body language and how leaders are perceived, you may want to think about how you can adapt in different situations and environments. It is not about pretending to be something that you're not. It is recognising that as a leader you need to be able to adapt your leadership style in different situations. Leaders who are high self-monitors adjust their attitude and behaviours to the demands of different situations[6]. They have a concern that their behaviour is socially appropriate for the situation, they are sensitive to social cues and have the ability to control their behaviour in response to those cues in order to influence the impression others have of them. High self-monitors try to fit in, and how this may play out with introverts who are high self-monitors is that they try to act extroverted. People who are low self-monitors have a 'take me as I am' attitude and act pretty much the same in all types of social settings. They don't see why they should fake it and pretend to be something that they're not.

By overly trying to control self-presentation (the process by which people monitor and control the impressions others form of them in social situations) we run the risk of letting our true selves slip out by way of non-verbal leakage[7]. That is, we say one thing, but our body language says another. This is something I have seen often in people who are introverts who try to act extroverted. You can see that it feels very uncomfortable for them.

If you are a low self-monitor, being rigid and not adapting your behaviour to the situation can affect how others perceive your leadership effectiveness. My client

Elizabeth, whom I mentioned in chapter 3 (who was an outward perfectionist), was a low self-monitor and didn't see why she should fake being something that wasn't her. She would sit disengaged in board meetings whilst her extroverted colleagues seemingly talked just for the sake of talking about things that she felt were unsubstantial. She thought that the meetings were a complete waste of her time and often didn't even attempt to feign interest. As a result, she appeared very disengaged, which put a barrier up between her and the rest of the senior leadership team.

Elizabeth recognised that if she was to develop a good working relationship with her colleagues, she would have to make an effort and engage with them. She didn't suddenly start acting extroverted and become loud and gregarious, though; that would have been a step too far for her. She stepped out of her comfort zone and started making an effort to engage in conversation with her colleagues, recognising that as extroverts they were doing what they loved to do best.

If you are a high self-monitor, the advantage is that, because of your adaptability, it increases your chances of success in getting on as a leader[8]. The downside is that it could give you a sense of self fragmentation and being known as a people pleaser, because you try to be all things to all people. Annie, whom I mentioned earlier in the chapter, very much tried to adapt and act more extroverted, but over time, she felt the pressure of trying to keep up this appearance. However, rather than forcing herself to act gregariously, perhaps Annie would have been better just being more social like my client Elizabeth by engaging with people on a one-to-one basis and in small groups. The upside of being a low self-monitor is that your consistency and commitment can lead to long-lasting relationships. The downside is that your inflexibility can negatively impact how you adapt to change as well as compromise your chances of success as a leader.

There needs to be a balance between having a 'take me as I am' attitude and adapting our behaviour according to the situation we are in because either taken to the extreme is beset with problems. I know that if I want to get ahead I have to adapt to the circumstances and environment as required. I do this without compromising who I am and what I stand for. I think Professor Brian Little sums it up very nicely in an interview with Professor Adam Grant where he says:

> "The conclusion I reach after giving a bunch of the research in this area is that I think, on balance, high self-monitoring is very adaptive. As long as it doesn't blend itself into what's called "aesthetic character disorder" where you are so imbued with the demands of the situation or the delights or the aesthetics of the situation that you will act in ways that go against your core values. There have been some politicians who have been accused of having aesthetic character disorder. That it, in turn, blends into a kind of insensitivity that can be downright dangerous."[9]

People who identify as being introverted often tell me that they never see an expectation on extroverts to adapt and fit in when they are in the minority in an introverted environment, yet introverts are always expected to adapt to extroverted environments. Even a search of the internet threw up only one article about how extroverts can thrive in an introverted environment. This tells me that the extrovert ideal is real. Some of you after reading this may be adamant that you will not adapt your behaviour and attitude to suit the environment, and that is ok. However, be aware that by being inflexible in this way may have an impact on your leadership progression.

If you do want to be more adaptable, self-reflection and feedback will enable you to become aware of your behaviour in different environments and situations, and help you to identify ways in which you can adapt. However, if it requires that you act in ways that are totally out of character for you and go against your core values, I suggest you ask yourself whether you really want to work in such an environment.

POWER POSES

With over 51 million views, Amy Cuddy is well known for her TED talk *Your Body Language May Shape Who You Are* where she talks about how our body language not only affects how others see us, but may also change how we see ourselves[10]. She said we shouldn't 'fake it until we make it' but 'fake it until we become it' – that is, we should keep doing it until it is imbedded in us. She became known worldwide for the power pose, i.e. that we feel more powerful when we pretend to be powerful and that by expanding our bodies in a power pose (arms held high and expanded or in a Wonder Woman pose with hands on hips) for 2 minutes before a stressful evaluative situation, we will bring a more powerful presence into what we need to do. She says that our bodies change the way we think and feel and the way we think and feel can change our behaviour, and our behaviour can change our outcomes. By using power poses to change our body language, it will change the end result.

There was some controversy about her claims in that other studies failed to replicate her findings and those of the other social psychologists she collaborated with. However, she later went on to publish a paper that offers plenty of evidence that power posing (adopting an expansive posture) makes people feel more powerful[11]. So whether it is a meeting, an interview or something else, the next time you are in a situation where your performance will be evaluated, go somewhere where you can be alone for 2 minutes, close the door, and strike a power pose.

When entering any situation where you want to appear confident, it is good to do a quick body scan to give yourself an awareness of how you are presenting yourself. You may want to get someone to video record you doing a presentation delivering a talk so that you can see how you present yourself in those sorts of situations. This will enable you to see where you can make improvements.

I remember years ago practising at delivering a workshop in front of some friends and the feedback I got was that I fidgeted from side to side at times, which could be a bit distracting to some people. I wasn't even aware that I did this. However, with that awareness I was then mindful of how I stood when delivering talks and presentations in the future. And now, when I watch video recordings of myself, I don't see myself fidgeting from side to side the way I did back then.

There are many other nuances like this, which some of us do when we are in situations where all eyes are glaring intently upon us. By bringing them into your awareness, it means that you can be mindful about what you can do differently.

I'M SORRY BUT...

"I'm sorry to bother you but..." and "I'm sorry to be a pain but..." are words often used by the apologetic woman which, with passive undertones, don't instil confidence in her leadership abilities. And it is not just introverted women who do this. Extroverted women do it too. Apologising in the way described because you don't want to cause offence can have the effect that you are not worthy of the other person's time, or that they are so much better or more important than you. If you want to exude executive presence, ditch the apologetic talk.

Although women are often stereotyped as being more apologetic than men, there is actually little empirical evidence to back this up. What one study shows, though, is that when men think they have done something wrong they do actually apologise just as often as when women think they've done something wrong[12]. But with men, they think they've not done as many things that they need to apologise for. According to this particular study, women have a lower threshold as to what constitutes offensive behaviour that they need to apologise for. A possible reason given for this is that women are more concerned with the emotional experiences of others and in promoting harmony in their relationships. This was a two part study and in study one participants wrote daily in a diary all offences they committed and whether they offered an apology.

Women reported apologising more than men, and not only that, reported that they had committed more offences. They found no gender difference in the proportion of offences that caused them to apologise. They found that men apologise less than women because their threshold as to what is an offence is higher. In the second study, they asked participants to evaluate both imaginary and recalled offences. Men rated the offences less severely than the women did and the different ratings of severity predicted both judgments of whether an apology was deserved and actual apology behaviour.

Harriet Lerner PhD has been studying the subject of apologies for many years and says that over apologising could be about many things[13]. Such things as low self-esteem, a diminished sense of entitlement, unconsciously wanting to avoid disapproval or criticism, shame, wanting to please and so on. From my experience, I've seen women become overly apologetic in situations where they need to deliver awkward, difficult or challenging messages, or something that is not favourable to the recipient of their communication. Or where they doubt themselves or their ability and think they're not as good as the person they are apologising to. What this overly apologetic approach does is make the person come across as timid, uncertain, lacking assertiveness, or as faltering. All of which doesn't bode well for being seen as a confident leader.

I'm sure you don't approach your children (if you have them) after a tiring, stressful day of them playing up and creating a mess and say, "I'm sorry to bother you, but would you mind tidying your bedroom?" I'm pretty sure you would approach the subject in a more assertive manner in order to get the outcome you want, namely tidy bedrooms and a peaceful evening. If you want to be seen to have executive presence, be mindful of overly apologetic talk and how that portrays you as a leader. When faced with an awkward situation that you need to address, try ditching the 'sorry but' at the start of your sentence. And if you're worried that the person may not like you because of what you say, or because you may inconvenience them, if it leads to a better outcome, does it really matter? Besides, if they respond negatively, they're not rejecting you, they're just not pleased with what you have communicated to them.

Rather than spending hours in front of your computer pondering how you're going to start that email, or taking ages mustering up the courage to broach that awkward conversation, visualise what you would like the outcome to be. Then, having visualised the outcome, ask yourself what it is that you can do to achieve that outcome, then go ahead and do it.

COMMANDING THE ROOM

Being able to command the room enhances your influence as a leader. It means gaining the respect and attention of those in the room so that they want to sit up and listen to what you have to say. When you think of leaders you have worked with who have been able to command the room, who comes to mind? What is it about them that causes you to pay attention and listen to them intently? When you think of leaders who don't command the room, what is it about them that doesn't grab your attention and causes you to switch off? What can you take from that reflection and apply to your situation?

There are certain things you can do prior to entering the room such as preparation, knowing who is likely to be there, and being clear about the objectives for the situation you are about to encounter. What outcome do you want from the situation? What outcome do other people want?

There's nothing worse than arriving late at a meeting or event where you want to make your mark. Whilst there may be a genuine unavoidable reason for being late, the mere fact you are late is likely to rub away at some of your gravitas. It also may make you feel flustered and like you are not in control. Arrive early, but in the event that you do get there late, rather than rushing in looking flustered and disorganised, give yourself a moment to compose yourself before entering the room. Give your apologies and then sit down calmly.

Arriving early will give you more of a sense of control. People who are able to command a room come across as if they are in control. Whether they really are or not is another matter. We can't see what is going on inside for someone – we only see the image that they portray to us. Put into practice what is covered in chapter 4 on speaking and chapter 6 on networking.

Connect with the people in the room and build rapport. Be interested in what others have to say and be fully present when speaking to them. Be positive and have an optimistic outlook. People are more likely to gravitate to you this way. If you are the one leading the event, maintain control and don't let the larger-than-life personalities try to steal your show.

YOUR PERSONAL BRAND

Many women are not sure what their personal brand is, why they need to be concerned about it, or they don't even know what is meant by the term personal brand.

Jeff Bezos, CEO of Amazon, is credited as saying, 'your brand is what people say about you when you're not in the room' which I think sums it up nicely. What do people say about you when you're not in the room? Is what they say what you want to be known for? Do you even know what they say about you?

Our values go to the core of who we are and they define what matters most to us and what it is that we stand for. Do you know what your values are? Be clear about what your values are, and make sure that you align with your values and are able to articulate them.

If you want to know what people say about you when you are not in the room, get feedback. Ask 5-10 of your colleagues, friends and family how they would describe you as a person. What are your qualities? What is it that they like about you? What is it that they are not keen on and why? The way that we see ourselves is not often how others see us. Although you may see yourself as being a certain way, others may see you as being totally different. A woman who attended one of my career change workshops was employed as a caseworker and was surprised that her colleagues saw her as a leader because she didn't see herself that way. When we explored the feedback they had given her, it became clear why they viewed her like this. She was then able to incorporate this into how she described herself and the sort of roles she went on to look for.

If you get feedback that is not favourable, don't be dismayed or upset. Use it to increase your self-awareness about the impact your behaviour has on others. If you don't like what you hear, modify your behaviour. Remember that this is how people perceive you. In reality, the women I work with are very modest and tend to view themselves less favourably than how others do so they are pleasantly surprised at the feedback they get.

What are the things that you are good at? What skills do you have? How are you utilising your strengths and skills? How are they displayed in the way that you work and the way that you conduct yourself? Identify your strengths and your skills and be able to clearly articulate them and how you use them.

What is your personal story and how does it shape who you are today? What value does your previous experience bring to what you have to offer? Does your story create interest in you? How does your story differentiate you from others? All the previous points feed into your personal story which represents your personal brand. How can you articulate this succinctly whilst creating an emotional connection that lets others believe that you can make a difference that will positively impact them?

Applying the above will help you to form your personal brand. Once your personal brand is defined and you are able to articulate it, live it and own it. Let it become what people say about you when you are not in the room.

YOUR APPEARANCE

Whilst I'm not a personal stylist, I will touch on appearance. Appearance does matter if you want to have executive presence. I once met a woman who had been overlooked for promotion to senior manager. The quality and standard of her work could not be faulted, but she wasn't considered senior leadership material. Just going by her appearance alone, I could see why. There were tweaks she could make in the way that she dressed if she was to be taken as a serious contender for senior leadership.

Some organisations have a grooming policy, and some have an unspoken dress code. There is a lot to be said about dressing for the role that you want, and the same can be said about dressing to exude a leadership presence. Dress appropriately for the environment that you are in. That said, I don't condone any discriminatory practices when it comes to a person's appearance. Wearing the right cut of clothes to suit your body shape and the colours that suit your tone can make a world of difference.

I once had a colleague and I noticed over a period of time that there was something different about her, but I couldn't put my finger on what it was. She appeared more attractive, exuding a new level of confidence, and people were paying attention to what she had to say in ways they'd never done before. One day I asked her what it was that was different about her and she told me that her colours had been done. She was now only wearing the range of colours that best suited her tone and the impact this had was amazing. In meetings people who had previously given her a hard time were being nice to her. Something as simple as the colours she wore made a significant difference to how others related to her.

DECISIVENESS

For many leaders who consider themselves to be introverted, being put on the spot to make an important decision or express their point of view can be challenging and uncomfortable. As a result, it may come across to those who don't get it that you don't have an opinion, or that you are indecisive. But for many of us this is certainly not the case. We like to think and reflect before making a decision or expressing our opinion. In her study of introverted leaders, Dr Oram found that many of the participants also preferred to think and reflect before making decisions[14].

When Georgia started a new role as VP for Human Resources, she told the team that she was introverted and that she made her best decisions by thinking and reflecting. She told them that if they wanted her to make a decision, to come to her a week or two in advance so she had time to think, reflect and do her research. She let them know if anyone wanted her to make an on-the-spot decision she could give them one, but she couldn't guarantee that it would be the best one.

Georgia set the tone from day one and people knew what to expect from her. She knew that she made her best decisions when she had time to think and reflect. This meant that when she did give her response, it was a sound decision. People came to know her as being loyal, supportive and right.

When the pressure is on in that moment, with all eyes glaring at you for a response, it can make things awkward, bringing on an internal panic, causing you to feel anxious inside. Whilst your preferred way of expressing an opinion or making an important decision may be to think and reflect before speaking, as a leader, there will be times when you do need to respond on the spot, particularly if there is an imminent health and safety risk. Having some strategies to deal with these challenging moments will enable you to get through in a way that means important matters get dealt with effectively and swiftly, even though it's uncomfortable or doesn't play to your strengths.

BUY SOME TIME

Fast is not always better and if it is a situation that is not life threatening, or where there is not an imminent risk, buy yourself some time. Let people know that you have a view, express your initial thoughts and let them know that you will get back to them with a more carefully considered opinion. You may be going against the grain, but hold your ground. Be the one to influence the team on the importance of having a collective view that takes into account the different decision-making styles of the personalities at the table.

SEEK THE OPINION OF THOSE YOU TRUST

Who are the ones in the room whose views you trust (including those who have differing opinions to you)? How do their views resonate with you? Listen to what they have to say. Knowing that you have always respected and trusted their views (even if you have not always agreed with them), by gaining their insight will help you to make a more informed decision. At the end of the day, you have the final say, but getting different perspectives will help to clarify your decision.

IDENTIFY CRISIS HANDLING SCENARIOS

If you are experienced at what you do, you will be able to anticipate the types of problems that are likely to occur that will require on-the-spot decisions. Knowing that on-the-spot decision making is not your preferred style or how you make your best decisions, develop your personal emergency response kit. Go through possible scenarios that could arise (or think about ones that have arisen in the past) and think about how you could deal with them in the best possible way. That way, when a real situation occurs, you will already have an idea of how to respond, making it easier for you to make a quick decision.

WEIGH UP THE PROS AND CONS

I once had a situation where I needed to decide whether or not to evacuate the building of one of my business units following a significant oil leak at one of the locations that was heated by oil. The fumes quickly seeped through the building, affecting staff, customers and stakeholders. Advice given to me by health and safety advisers was conflicting. I was told by one party that the fumes were not toxic and that there was no risk to health. Other advice was not quite so reassuring.

The people in the building were complaining about the strong smell from the fumes. I had to make a quick decision as to whether to bear the cost and inconvenience of evacuating, against the risk of letting people remain in the building. Evacuating would mean a delay to court hearings, prisoners having to be securely relocated, victims and witnesses being inconvenienced, not to mention everyone else in the building.

Weighing up the pros and cons, I decided to evacuate, even though there was a possibility that the fumes, although unpleasant and uncomfortable, would have no impact on health. Without all the evidence before me to make a carefully considered and informed decision, to me the health and safety of those in the building was my paramount concern. So my advice would be to quickly weigh up the pros and cons of your situation and make a decision based on that.

TRUST YOUR INTUITION

In an important situation where you have no choice but to make an on-the-spot decision, trust your intuition. Your intuition will be based on your developed experience of doing the role, previous situations and the organisation. It won't just be based on a haphazard guess. If you can combine your intuition with some analysis, then even better, because as researcher Bjørn T. Bakken found in his study, those who normally prefer combining intuitive decisions with analysis made the best decisions in crisis situations[15]. Whilst you may not have the time to do much analysis because you don't have all the information to hand, you can adjust as you receive more information and are able to better analyse. Practise the crisis-handling scenarios identified above to develop a flexible decision-making style that enables you to combine your intuition with analysis.

Whilst your preferred way of making decisions or expressing your opinion may be to pause, think and reflect before you act, as a leader there will be times when you have to go against this and you will need to act and lead in ways that you are not comfortable with. Developing yourself in the ways suggested above will assist you in making it easier to make those on-the-spot, important decisions. If you find those situations where you need to make on-the-spot decisions draining, identify ways of re-energising following such occasions, such as scheduling solitude time afterwards that will enable you to recharge.

We've covered quite a lot in this chapter and rather than trying to look at how you can improve everything all at once, you may find it easier to break it down and start with whichever you think will be the most beneficial for you.

SELF-REFLECTION EXERCISE

- What areas do you need to work on to develop your leadership presence?
- What can you do to develop these areas?
- Which area will you tackle first?
- Who can you ask to give you feedback as to what your leadership presence is like now, and then once you've taken action?

8 | Quiet Influence

The ability to influence is important as a leader, and it's not just about getting people to do what you want. Just because someone is a leader, it does not automatically mean that they have the ability to influence. However, leaders can strongly influence the performance of those they lead as well as workplace attitudes[1]. The Oxford Dictionary defines influence as 'the capacity to have an effect on the character, development, or behaviour of someone or something, or the effect itself'. In *Influence: A Primer (Building Blocks of Emotional Intelligence Book 8)* psychologist Daniel Goleman describes influence as being the ability to have a positive impact on others, and to persuade or convince them to gain their support[2]. People who are influential are persuasive and engaging and can get buy-in from key people.

Influencing is not about being manipulative, coercing, forcing, tricking, deceiving, or brainwashing. Whilst these may get other people to do what you want them to do, they will not be doing it willingly. It is far better to have people come alongside you willingly than forcibly, a bit like the Aesop fable, *The North Wind and the Sun*. In this fable, the north wind boasted that there was power in strength, whereas the sun argued that there was greater power in gentleness, so they decided to have a contest to see who could get a man to take off his jacket. As much as the wind provided pressure to force the man to take off his coat, he clung on to it more tightly; whereas the sun shone until the man got so hot he willingly took it off.

If you are a leader who focuses on what people do wrong as opposed to giving praise, or the type of old school leader who orders people around in a command and control style, it is likely that you will not influence people to buy in to your ideas and ways of working. They may do what you want them to do, but it is more likely to be because they have to, not because they do it with a willing attitude. In the long term, this can lead to disengagement, and when people are disengaged, they are not going to be at their best.

INFLUENCE RATHER THAN PERSUASION

I have often heard sales people boast that they could sell sand in the desert, meaning that their sales techniques are so good that even someone living in a desert who is surrounded by sand would still buy sand from them. Getting someone to buy something from you in that context is persuasion. Or rather, selling somebody something that they do not need through persuasion is manipulation.

Whilst there is need for both persuasion and influence in the skill repertoire of a leader, if you want people to buy in to your vision and ideas in an empowered way, the ability to influence needs to be part of who you are and what you do. Persuading is like commanding someone to do something. They may not necessarily want to do it but do it because they have been commanded to. It is better for you as a leader to have people who are inspired to act and willingly want to support your aim. They are more likely to be happier, more motivated and more productive than someone who goes along with what you want them to do purely because they have been commanded to do it, even though they may not buy in to it.

As a leader, good influencing skills are required when it comes to implementing change, shaping opinion, interviews, engagement, helping others to motivate themselves, getting buy in to your vision and ideas, and negotiating. I have come across many introverted women who have a misconception of influencing, and because they don't consider themselves to be charismatic, believe they lack the ability to be a good influencer. This is mainly because of the perception that charismatic people are good in social situations, whereas many introverts do not necessarily thrive in highly social environments. It is when it comes to wanting to be seen as influential that many of the introverted women I have worked with or spoken to have felt the need to put on an extroverted persona. Over time, they realise that doing this is to their detriment.

Whilst some charisma is required as a leader, too much charisma is actually bad for leadership[3]. In any event, influencing is much more than bringing people along with you because of your charisma. When it comes to influencing, the objective is for those you want to influence to believe in what you want to do on an intellectual and emotional level.

SELF-AWARENESS

Leaders with self-awareness and emotional self-control are better able to influence others and cultivate effective relationships[4]. Having an awareness of the impact you or the decisions you make have on others means you will be more aware of how to present what you want people to buy in to, in a way that is better received. If the environment you work in is more geared towards an extroverted way of being, and you have the typical characteristics associated with introversion, a lack of self-awareness could mean that your preferred way of being doesn't create the engagement that is needed to be influential. Leaders who are equipped with the emotional self-awareness and self-control to manage themselves while being adaptable, positive, and empathic, can express their ideas in a way that will appeal to others.

The organisation that I was a leader in had been through significant changes and was about to go through even more. There was change apathy amongst the teams and taking an approach that did not engage them and which they did not buy in to would have made the change processes difficult. One of the change initiatives I was leading on was the centralisation of a particular administrative process from 22 locations to one. With an awareness that this change would not be well received by either employees or stakeholders, I established a working group comprising of different grades of employees from different locations within the area, so that those actually doing the work could be involved. They would have a direct input on how the change was implemented, the designing of a new standard operating procedure, and they would be spokespersons to feed back to their peers. This was well received, and because of their involvement and buy in, what could have been a nightmare to implement resulted in a smooth transition. It also resulted in me getting feedback in my appraisal that I had demonstrated excellent change management skills.

RAPPORT

To build trust as a leader, there needs to be rapport between yourself and the people you want to influence. It is key to building strong connections, and if you are to make an impact and influence others, develop the rapport. Rapport is the sense of connection you get when you meet someone you like and trust. This is where extroverts have the advantage because they are typically better at building rapport than introverts[5]. Korrina Duffy and Tanya Chartrand found in a study they did that where there is a motivation to do so, extroverts mimic more than introverts as a way to build rapport. Researchers have found that immediate social bonding between strangers is dependent on mimicry[6]. When a stranger mimics someone's verbal and non-verbal expressions of someone, that person they are mimicking views them more favourably[7].

To develop rapport with someone you're meeting for the first time, find common ground. Find a mutual interest or something that you have in common that can be the focus of your initial conversation. This will enable you to warm to each other and open up the conversation. Asking open questions, listening and asking more open questions enables you to then build on the conversation and allows the conversation to flow. Many introverts don't like making small talk but, as mentioned previously, small talk is the segue to the more meaningful conversations which many of us tend to prefer.

LISTENING

Listening is a key factor in being able to influence, and in the report *The Role of Listening in Interpersonal Influence* researchers found that listening had a positive effect on influence beyond the impact of the communication of beliefs and opinions. Their research highlighted that when it comes to influencing, listening matters above and beyond verbal and non-verbal communication and that listening combines with verbal and non-verbal communication to shape influence[8].

People like to be listened to and to feel that their voice has been heard. Unfortunately, many leaders are not good at listening to the people that they lead. We spend 70-80% of our waking time communicating, and of that time 45% is spent listening. The remaining is spent speaking 30%, reading 16% and writing 9%[9]. Considering that the bulk of our communication is spent listening, why do so many people do it so ineffectively? We can learn so much about a person, clients, people's needs, what makes them tick, what turns them off, our environments, and so on... all through listening.

How many times do you engage in conversation with one of your team members but your mind is racing ahead, thinking about the hundreds of emails sitting in your inbox waiting for a reply? Or that important meeting you've got coming up in a couple of hours? Or that report with the deadline looming? Or thinking about what you're going to have for dinner that evening? With so many competing demands and distractions vying for our attention, it is far too easy to not be mindful when listening. How many times do you interrupt a person when they are speaking or try to finish someone's sentence with your own words, rather than letting them use theirs?

When you do this, the conversation doesn't necessarily go in the direction that the person who is speaking intends. By imposing your words on them, you are expressing your perspective rather than them expressing theirs. Most people probably do this without even realising it. Likewise, the person being listened to may not even be aware that this is happening. All they know is that they don't feel as if their voice has been heard and understood.

Have you ever had a conversation with someone with a more dominant personality who literally took over the conversation, interjecting their views and opinions so that the conversation became all about them? How did it leave you feeling? Did you leave the conversation inspired by their influence? Or did it drain the energy out of you and leave you feeling unheard?

Active listening so that someone feels like they are being heard can be very empowering for them. And even if the outcome is not one they initially wanted, they are more likely to be engaged if they feel that their voice has been heard. Effective listening is a key component of being influential, and being able to influence is essential if you are to be an effective leader.

Through listening you can also learn a lot about yourself by what is not said, not just by what is said. A good leader is self-aware. They are aware of the impact they have on others. They are aware of how and why they respond to situations the way that they do. As mentioned, this self-awareness enables them to adapt to situations accordingly. Self-awareness comes through self-reflection, and listening is a key element of self-reflection and requires listening to yourself as well as to the feedback (both verbal and non-verbal) from others.

If your mind is not present in the conversation, the other person can tell and is not going to feel like they are being listened to. Whilst you might not think that they can tell that you are wondering what you're going to have for dinner that evening, you are mistaken because they can! Whilst they can't tell exactly what it is that you're thinking about, they can tell that your mind is distracted.

There is a lot that you can pick up about a person through the non-verbal communication they make when you are talking with them. This requires observing the other person's body language, including posture, facial expressions and hand movements. Be aware of whether the other person makes eye contact with you or whether they continuously avoid looking at you. When they do make eye contact, observe how comfortable or uncomfortable they look. Ask yourself what your observations tell you and what you can learn from them. Be mindful of cultural and other differences that you may be misinterpreting.

Be aware of your emotions and feelings and the impact these can have on your conversations. We often respond to conversations based on our emotions which may or may not be a good way to respond. If you yourself are stressed or anxious, you may not respond to a conversation rationally. In such situations, explore the feelings that are invoked in you during the conversation. If the conversation (or the person) makes you feel uncomfortable, what is the reason for that? An awareness of your own emotions and how to manage them will help you to listen effectively.

A good communicator is able to get their message across in a way that is understood by the person receiving it. To be an effective listener it needs to work both ways and requires that you understand the message that the person you are speaking to is relaying to you – so listen in order to understand. We often hear what people are saying to us but don't necessarily understand, and rather than seeking clarification, we put our own interpretation on what they're saying. This may look nothing like the message that the person wants to get across to us.

Seek clarification on what the person is saying to you so that you understand exactly what it is that they are trying to say. Use paraphrasing as a way to show that you are listening to them. Use non-verbal communication and nuances that confirm that you are not only listening but that you also understand.

Not everyone is naturally a good listener. Some people think that they are good at it when they are not. Listening, however, is a skill that can be developed. Self-awareness and practice will help you to achieve this. If you want to be considered a good, effective leader and be influential and you are not a good listener, it is a skill that I highly recommend you learn how to develop. Listening to different perspectives and letting those differing perspectives feel like they've been heard is more likely to create dialogue that builds consensus[10].

EMPATHY

Empathy takes listening to another level through hearing the feelings behind what is being said. It is the ability to understand another person's experience, emotions, and perspective. When you are able to empathise, it helps the other person to feel valued, connected, and understood. It helps to build trust. We often hear the term 'walking in another man's shoes' being used to describe empathy. Being able to empathise with those you want to influence will help you to be influential. It is not necessarily agreeing with people, but it is showing an understanding of their feelings and needs.

Empathy will enable you to understand the impact of your decisions on those who are affected. It is wanting to understand another person, not just for the sake of making them think you want to. It is actually caring about understanding them. Leaders who are high in empathy are better at keeping employees engaged[11]. Although you are able to empathise, it does not mean that because you understand other people's emotions and perspective, you have to then try to please them if they disagree with you. It means that you will be able to take their perspective and the impact on them into consideration when making decisions. By doing so, you will be better placed to identify what could help them to understand your perspective.

Empathy is developed by sensing what others feel without them speaking it. Their tone of voice, body language, facial expressions and other non-verbal cues can help us to understand how a person may be feeling if we are observant enough. In order to empathise, we need to be self-aware and be aware of our own feelings and not let our emotions be so strong that we are not able to pick up on what may be going on for the other person.

Empathy is something I often help my clients with when they are leading others through some sort of change, or they are dealing with what they consider difficult and challenging people. This could be members of their team, their manager, stakeholders or even customers. When it comes to difficult and challenging individuals, my clients' emotions are often quite strong in a negative way about the behaviour of the individuals concerned. As such, they may be viewing the situation in a one-dimensional way, i.e. that the other person is at fault. Helping them to understand the perspective of the individual or individuals helps them to find solutions to better manage the relationship, creating better outcomes.

In a conversation with psychologist Daniel Goleman, Paul Ekman, a world expert on emotions and our ability to read and respond to them in others, talks about there being three types of empathy, namely cognitive, emotional and compassionate[12]. Cognitive empathy, also known as perspective taking, enables us to know how the other person feels and how they may be thinking. This kind of empathy is good when negotiating or when wanting to motivate other people. Paul Ekman mentions a study at the University of Birmingham that found that managers who were good at this sort of empathy got the best effort from those who worked for them.

There is a dark side to this type of empathy, though, as can be seen in leaders who are narcissists, Machiavellians and sociopaths (known as the Dark Triad) and lack sympathy towards their 'victims'. It can lead to manipulation and getting people to do what they want using unethical means or for an unethical cause. In *Social Intelligence: The New Science of Human Relationships*, Daniel Goleman states: 'Modern society, glorifying me-first motives and worshipping celebrity demigods of greed unleashed and vanity idealised, may be inadvertently inviting these types to flourish.'[13]

Emotional empathy is where you feel a connection to what the other person is experiencing emotionally and physically, and it helps to develop an emotional connection between you. You not only understand how they feel, you also understand why they feel that way and are able to respond in an appropriate way so that they feel like you understand. Emotions greatly influence the decisions we make and as such, you are more likely to be influential when there is an emotional connection than when there is not.

A downside to emotional empathy is that too much focus on other people's distressful emotions can be draining and lead to stress if you are unable to detach yourself. If not managed, it can lead to depression, hopelessness and burnout.

Compassionate empathy is where we not only understand what a person is going through and feel it with them, but where we are also moved to help them if needed. People who are high in emotional empathy are those most moved to help[14]. In terms of how this relates to influencing, this means helping the other person/people to understand and come around to your way of thinking. Or, if necessary, identifying what needs to be put in place to support them or help them to adjust.

Putting yourself in the shoes of the other person, so to speak, imagine what may be going on for them and why they respond to you in the way that they do. A way in which you can demonstrate empathy is by way of mirroring[15]. This involves repeating back to the person what they are saying in your own words. Capture not just their thoughts, but also what they are feeling. If they indicate that you are incorrect, try again until you get it right. In order to help them open up about what is going on for them, ask open questions and listen to the answer. Questions that begin what, where, when, who, why and how mean they have to respond with more than just a yes or no answer. The benefits of empathy when trying to influence are two-fold; not only does the other person feel understood, but also there is a sense of emotional attunement. This can help to diffuse hostile situations and it also helps to establish trust.

TRUST

To be influential, people need to trust you. They need to have confidence in you and in your ability and to be assured that what you want is the best way forward. They need to believe in you. You need to develop your knowledge, skills and experience, demonstrate confidence in what you say and do, and establish credibility. When those you lead trust you, they are more likely to be committed to achieving the team/ organisation goals and objectives.

A lack of trust leads to people being afraid or angry[16]. It can cause them to jump to conclusions, distort reality or ignore facts. If people do not trust you as a leader, they will be resistant to what you say and do, making it difficult for you to influence them. In order for people to trust you, you have to prove yourself credible to them. To establish credibility, demonstrate knowledge and expertise at what you do on a consistent basis. Be clear about your values and be aligned with them, and be a person of integrity in what you say and what you do. Develop and nurture relationships and show respect to others. Be accountable, and when you are wrong, admit you are wrong.

COMMUNICATING YOUR MESSAGE

If because of your introverted nature your preference is to close the door, sit behind a screen and do your communication via email, you might want to switch things up a bit. Whilst that may be your preferred way of communicating, it might not be the preferred way of receiving communication for those you want to influence. By adapting your communication style, even though you may find it uncomfortable, you will have different methods of getting your message across that connect with the people you want to influence.

A new statutory obligation meant that a particular type of work had to be fast tracked through the system, working in conjunction with partner agencies. Wanting to communicate the message and the process that needed to be taken, I got creative in the way that I delivered the message. I designed posters with a visual image that represented the type of work that this related to and placed them in strategic, eye-catching places throughout the offices. I arranged a team building afternoon with the different departments to coincide with the posters having been up for a few weeks. Part of the team building event included a quiz on the requirements and obligations concerning the new processes, to test how well my communication had been understood. The responses to the questions assured me that my message had been well received and understood – and not only that, we all had fun!

Clear and consistent communication and ensuring your message is understood is necessary if you are to be influential. This is particularly so if you are wanting to influence change. It is often when there is change going on in an organisation that a lack of communication starts the gossip-mongering and speculative rumours about what is happening, as people draw their own conclusions. The sooner you can communicate the plan to your teams, the better it is for everybody. People would rather hear bad news than no news and be left to draw their own conclusions. In the absence of clarity about what the future holds, let your communication focus on the positives.

Communicate what is going on frequently to keep your teams updated and apprised of the situation. If they are not kept informed, they are likely to start guessing and invariably imagine the worst. And it may be that the worst is going to happen, and if this is likely, maintain optimism and help them to see the good that can come out of the situation, even if it means that some of them may have to leave the organisation. If you are a leader that manages other leaders, make sure that your leadership team are fully apprised of what is going on, that you are all singing from the same hymn sheet and sending out the same communication messages.

SELLING THE BENEFITS

Leaders are sales people. Even though you may not sell a product or service directly to the customer, selling is an aspect of what you do. Selling your ideas, your vision or initiatives, and wanting them to be well received. In *To Sell Is Human: The Surprising Truth About Persuading, Convincing and Influencing Others*, Daniel Pink talks about having clarity about what you are offering and why who you are selling to does not want to buy[17]. In any situation where you want to influence others, be clear as to the benefits of what you are putting forward. And if there are no benefits to the individual(s) concerned, be clear as to why what you are putting forward is needed.

Anticipate concerns and questions they may have in advance, and identify solutions and answers so that you can raise these and deal with their concerns before they have an opportunity to do so. When centralising the administrative process that I mentioned earlier, I anticipated that there would be lots of resistance from a particular group of stakeholders. A briefing was sent out to them setting out how the transition would take place, with contact details of whom they should contact if they had any concerns. I also held meetings with them to answer any questions that they had.

Whilst this change was not something that they particularly wanted, nor were there any significant benefits to them, they were able to understand the reason why my organisation needed to implement this change.

PUSH OR PULL?

It will depend on the nature of what it is that you want to influence whether you need to adopt a push or pull approach. Push involves persuasive reasoning, and pull involves being collaborative and visionary.[18]

A push approach is necessary in situations such as where there is a sense of urgency, a safety or security risk, where you're the expert, or where there are inexperienced staff.

A pull approach is useful when you want others to come up with their own innovative ideas, express their views and opinions, and when you want to tap into their emotions and help them visualise the desired outcome.

It is important to know when a push or pull approach is needed. The wrong approach will either make you come across as being too heavy handed or appear indecisive.

Assertiveness

When you want to influence, don't be passive or aggressive, but be assertive. Psychologist Dr Randy Paterson offers a good analogy that explains the differences. He likens it to being on a stage. For the passive person, the world is allowed on the stage but the passive individual's role is to be the audience and supporter for everyone else. For the aggressive person, they're allowed on stage but they want centre stage and spend most of their time shoving others off. For the assertive person, everyone is welcome on the stage[19].

A passive style of communicating avoids conflict. It involves going along with the crowd and not voicing your opinion until others have voiced theirs. Passive people don't like giving negative feedback or criticising, and they don't say things that will result in getting disapproval from others. As a result of being passive, we give other people control of our lives, as if they are more important than us. People with an aggressive style of communicating want to be in control, having other people submit to them and using intimidation to control their behaviour.

A passive aggressive style is a combination of the two. It is getting your own way (through an aggressive form of communication), but justifying the behaviour and not taking responsibility for the aggressive way you've gone about it. Assertiveness is about having an open and honest exchange in which you respect everyone's wishes and desires. It is about being in charge of your behaviour and decisions, whilst recognising that other people are in charge of theirs. It is about deciding whether or not to go along with others, or expressing your preference for others to go along with you[20.]

Which category do you fall into? If you are the audience/supporter, or constantly pushing everyone off stage, what can you do to adapt your behaviour so that you are up there on the stage with everyone else?

SELF-REFLECTION EXERCISE

- How well do you really listen to others?
- What can you do to improve on the way you build rapport, trust and empathy?
- What improvements can you make to your verbal or written communication?
- What situation(s) do you need or want to influence other people in?
- What do you find difficult about influencing in these situations?
- What can you do differently in order to increase your influence?

9 | *Leading with Impact*

The difference between the success and failure of an organisation has a lot to do with the type of leaders it has and the leadership style that they adopt. That is why identifying your personal leadership style, and knowing how and when to adapt it, is important for you as a leader[1]. There are many leadership models and theories offering differing perspectives on what leadership is. They are not universal truths – rather, they offer a lens through which to view your situation as a leader. This allows you to explore, measure and assess a situation[2]. This final chapter does not subscribe to any one particular theory or model of leadership; what it does is draw from different theories, my 28 years' experience as a leader, my studies, the experience of leaders I have coached, and observations of leaders that I admire. I share my thoughts, insights and observations in ways to help provoke and challenge your thinking as a leader, so that you can reflect and identify ways in which you can lead with impact in your own authentic way.

START WITH YOUR BIG 'WHY'

If you want to be an impactful leader, the first place I suggest you start is to connect with your big 'why'. Having an intrinsic motivation for something that is bigger than you, that adds meaning to your life and that aligns with your values will enable you to be passionate about what you do. Passion for what you do and for the people is important to you being positively impactful. Not only does being passionate about what you do give you drive and motivation, but also people are attracted to and inspired by passion in others. When they are inspired, they are more likely to be engaged, motivated and perform at their best[3]. However, a word of caution here. Like with anything done to excess, too much passion can actually be a bad thing. It can make you blinkered and cloud your judgement, causing you to make ill-informed decisions.

My passion is the work that I do helping introverted women achieve optimal potential and become great leaders. I believe that everybody should be given equality of opportunity in the workplace and want to change the unfavourable narrative that exists towards introversion, women, and black and minority ethnics in the corporate environment. I am particularly passionate about helping women who lack self-belief and don't see how great they are. I find it very rewarding helping them to peel off the layers that cloud their perception of themselves, to develop their self-belief and to go on and soar.

Your big 'why', that sense of meaning and purpose you get from your work, has to come from within you[4]. That is why it is important to know your core values and for your values and the values of the organisation you work for to be aligned. Otherwise, if they are not, how will you stay motivated when the going gets tough? Also, if you're not passionate and energised by what you do, how can you expect those you lead to be?

In *Effective Leadership: How to Be a Successful Leader*, John Adair talks about how leadership often arises from having a vocation or a calling. He mentions how our calling is *'where our talents, interests, aptitudes and general personality find their optimum use in the service of others'*[5]. Adair quotes W. H. Auden's poem '*Sext*' which sums up beautifully how to tell if someone is doing something that they are passionate about:

> *'You need not see what someone is doing*
> *To know if it is his vocation.*
> *You have only to watch his eyes:*
> *A cook making sauce, a surgeon*
> *Making a primary incision,*
> *A clerk completing a bill of lading,*
> *Wear the same rapt expression,*
> *Forgetting themselves in a function.'*

What is it about what you do that you are passionate about? Do others see that you are passionate about what you do? How do your organisation's values align with yours?

BE VISIONARY AND THINK BIG PICTURE

Great leaders are visionary. Looking at the bigger picture, and developing a strategic outlook, they are able to clearly articulate the vision to those that they lead. Whether you are the CEO or a first line manager, develop a mental picture of where you want the organisation or your team to be in the next few years, and communicate it. Using vivid detail when communicating your vision is more powerful than when you don't. If leaders get across an evocative feeling of what the distant future could look like, it can foster individual and collective action. One study found that leaders use vague descriptions to communicate their vision that hardly inspire the people that they lead. However, by tapping into their imagination and vividly imagining real life situations in the distant future, translating this into words and communicating it, it captures attention and inspires people to take action[6].

In this study they use the example that seeing a measuring cup containing the amount of sugar that is in one can of fizzy drink deters more people from drinking fizzy drinks than reading about how many calories are in a can of them. The effect of this type of vivid detail is not just limited to when people see something first hand. It also applies to when they read text or hear words (the aim of which is to persuade) that bring to mind this type of vivid detail. In some ways I think that this is a bit like the warnings on cigarette packets. Over the years they have become more and more vivid both in images and the written word to more impactfully get across the dangers of smoking.

Having a vision will be your road map and give everyone a sense of direction. It also means that when you face setbacks, because you know the direction you are headed, it will be easier to pick yourself up and get back on track. Without a vision and with no sense of direction, when those setbacks come you may end up wandering aimlessly.

What is your vision? Where do you see your organisation, your team, and yourself in the next 3-5 years? What will you be doing? Who will you be working with? What will the organisation be doing? What does this look and feel like?

SELF-AWARENESS AND EMOTIONAL INTELLIGENCE

I have a saying that goes 'before you can lead others, you have to be able to lead yourself'. I believe that self-awareness is the most important quality for leaders because out of it flows so much more of what is required to be a great and effective leader. Unless you are aware of who, how and what you are being, you won't know how to be impactful. I hope that what I have written in previous chapters helps you to practise self-leadership and develop your self-awareness so that you make the kind of impact that you want to make through your work. As a leader you have the potential to be impactful in a positive way.

Because we may not often display enthusiastic animation as introverts, this can be misunderstood as aloofness, or not caring, which can create a distance between us and other people. I once had someone go behind my back and tell my manager that I didn't care during a particularly challenging time for my group. Fortunately, my manager knew me well enough to know that this couldn't be further from the truth. She knew I was passionate about my work and about the teams that I led.

Whilst I have covered authenticity in chapter 2, I will touch on it here because being your authentic self will help in your being impactful. When there is congruence between who you are and what you do, that is when you can become your best self. When you are being your best self, that is when you are at your optimum. You are more impactful when you are at your optimum.

When they first come for coaching, many of my clients tell me that they feel inauthentic. They think that they have to be something they are not which can make them feel trapped, and can feel suffocating. Doing this had become a vicious cycle for Denise. She put a lot of pressure on herself to act in ways that were not her. This in turn made her feel anxious. Because of the way she viewed herself, she strove for perfection in her work. Being a perfectionist was wearing her out and she felt exhausted. When I helped her to take the 'mask' off, accept herself as she was and be her authentic self, she felt free. She said it felt like a huge weight had been lifted from her shoulders.

Because we are at our best when we utilise our strengths, it goes without saying that if you want to be impactful as a leader, you need to utilise your strengths. Where you can, delegate those tasks that are areas of weakness for you to those for whom they are their strengths, as part of their development.

When I look back over my career at leaders who were great at what they did whom I admired, they all appeared to have high levels of emotional intelligence. When I look back at those leaders who were not engaging and who didn't inspire, they lacked emotional intelligence. Effective leadership rarely occurs when there is a lack of self-awareness and emotional intelligence[7]. There are many models of emotional intelligence but the one that I favour and have studied the most is the work of Daniel Goleman and Richard Boyatzis. With their model there are four domains, namely self-awareness, self-management, social awareness and relationship management.[8]

Within each of those four domains are 12 competencies, namely self-awareness (emotional self-awareness); self-management (emotional self-control, adaptability, achievement orientation, positive outlook); social awareness (empathy, organisational awareness); relationship management (influence, coach and mentor, conflict management, team work, inspirational leadership). Having a well-balanced range of the competencies enables a leader to deal with a variety of challenges that they are likely to encounter.

Thinking about yourself, which (if any) areas of emotional intelligence do you need to develop? What can you do to develop yourself in those areas?

HELPING OTHERS TO BE THEIR BEST

Gone are the days of the command and control style of leadership. If you want to be impactful as a leader and get the best out of your teams, you must be able to inspire them and you need to let them have autonomy in what they do. People who are being led want to feel valued[9]. You have to show them that they are valued and appreciated, and you have to let them utilise their strengths. Whilst we are each responsible for our own motivation and we can't motivate others, understanding those whom you lead and understanding what motivates them and what drives them means that you can create an environment that makes them want to motivate themselves and maximises them being at their optimal level.

I had three assistant managers who all wanted to compress their hours and work a four-day week. I was told that it couldn't work and that I shouldn't have leaders of that seniority who were not around full time. I was encouraged to only allow it for the one who had very young children, to accommodate her caring responsibilities. Whilst a mother myself, and whilst I understood where that advice was coming from, I was of the view that just because someone did not have children, or had children who were young adults, it did not mean that they too didn't want to have a better work-life balance. Neither did it mean that they should not be permitted to if conditions allowed for it, just because they didn't have small children.

Against the recommendation of my seniors, I agreed to all of them compressing their hours and working a four-day week on the basis that all three of them didn't take the same non-working day. Also, if there was anything of importance happening such as a meeting or event, they would need to rearrange their non-working day to accommodate. I also stipulated that between the four of us, only two people be off at any one time. This was a win/win situation that worked well. They all got what they wanted and I was able to accommodate their requests in a way that didn't compromise the business. The world of work has changed considerably and leaders need to be flexible and adaptable. You too need to be able to adapt to new and different ways of working, as well as enabling your teams to work in new and different ways as well.

Give people feedback and let them know how they are doing, whether it is good or bad. In the absence of feedback, people draw their own conclusions. I often find that when people do this they view themselves less favourably and at times question their impact and effectiveness. This can also go the other way in that they think they are doing a lot better than they actually are. Don't give them surprises at their end of year performance review; you should be having a dialogue with them throughout the year as to how well (or not) they are performing.

When giving feedback, be specific about what it relates to, give examples, and make it timely. Giving someone vague critical feedback months down the line does not help them and is not good leadership. I often find that this happens because a leader does not like having those difficult conversations. They either don't like upsetting people, or they see it as confrontation and don't like confrontation. The word confrontation in itself has negative, aggressive connotations and because of this, the word alone puts many women off. The thought of having to confront someone makes some women anxious. As a result, they end up saying nothing and the situation continues. Not only can this be stressful for the leader, it also has a negative impact on the rest of the team because the situation is not being dealt with, causing the leader to lose credibility as a leader amongst their teams. If you need to confront someone, rather than viewing it as a confrontation, look at it as an opportunity to help the other person understand your point of view.

Don't just be generous with the negative feedback either. Praise people when they have done something well, but don't be condescending or patronising about it. My client Elizabeth whom I mentioned in chapter 3 didn't get feedback from her manager, which helped to fuel the perfectionism and imposter syndrome. Elizabeth's manager was an introvert too. Additionally, because she was an outward perfectionist with a very high standard, Elizabeth didn't give her team members praise when they had achieved results. She saw it as them only doing what they were paid to do so never thought to praise them. Coaching helped her to see the need to praise her team and the impact it would have on their motivation. As uncomfortable as it was for her, she set about praising them. She also started having consistent monthly one-to-one meetings with them and adopted a coaching style at those meetings, letting them set their own goals as opposed to her imposing goals on them.

Studies show that introverted leaders don't empower their team members as easily as extroverted leaders[10]. Help your team members to set intrinsically motivating goals because people who do so are more likely to achieve them than people whose goals are not intrinsically motivating and on whom goals have been imposed. Give them as much autonomy as possible to achieve their goals.

Be concerned with their wellbeing and create an environment that encourages it. We are more likely to be at our optimum when we take care of our wellbeing. As a leader, ensure that you are modelling behaviour that is conducive to this because what you do will set the tone for others to follow. If you make yourself available 24/7, even if you don't expect your teams to do so, they may feel under pressure to stay late, or take work home with them because that is what you do. Be mindful of how those unhealthy work habits can impact on your team.

Maura Thomas is a trainer on individual and corporate productivity, attention management and work-life balance, and says, '*A frantic environment that includes answering emails at all hours doesn't make your staff more productive. It just makes them busy and distracted.*'[11] I used to hate it when I'd cleared my mailbox on a Friday evening and then went in on a Monday morning to a barrage of emails that had been sent by someone from head office who had worked over the weekend. The more senior you get, the bigger the responsibility and the more likely that you will work out of hours. However, don't make this a habit, and most definitely don't make your teams feel that they have to either. On those times when I did work out of hours, I would schedule my emails to go out at different times throughout the day so that my teams didn't get bombarded with emails from me as soon as they came in, or see emails sent from me late in the evening and feel that they had to work that late too.

If empowering your team is something that you don't find easy, what can you do to step out of your comfort zone and empower them? If you are not yet in a leadership position, what can you do to encourage your colleagues to motivate themselves and to be at their best?

DON'T MICROMANAGE

If you give your team members autonomy and trust them to do what they are paid to do, you will see how well they get on and do it. When we micromanage, we are demonstrating that we don't trust our teams, and not only that, we are showing our insecurities as well. The effects of micromanaging and a lack of trust leads to frustrated teams who will only live up to your expectation because of the way that you treat them.

Micromanaging someone can stifle their creativity and innovation, and stifle their development. This in turn could start to affect their performance and productivity levels because they are not given the autonomy to think and act for themselves. It is no surprise that organisations that have a high level of micromanaging also have lower employee engagement and a high turnover of staff. This is not only costly from a financial perspective, it is also costly from a labour-intensive perspective, and it negatively impacts morale and puts added pressure on you as the leader.

A good leader will ensure that those they lead are clear about what they need to do, and where they are not, give them the necessary support to bring them up to speed. Where the person's performance is a cause for concern, an effective leader will address this promptly, rather than brushing it under the carpet and burying their head in the sand. A command and control leadership style does not bring out the best in people and stifles creativity and decision making. You will get the best out of your teams if they are intrinsically motivated, as opposed to the threatening authority that a command and control leadership style brings.

Understanding the different dynamics at play with people who are different to you will help you to understand the individuals better and know how to get the best from them. In doing so, you make conditions more conducive to them being their best possible selves. Gillian had a manager on her team whom she thought was always trying to undermine her. This team member would often go above Gillian directly to the CEO with her ideas and to let him know about what she was doing or what she had achieved. As a result, Gillian started micromanaging the person which caused friction in their relationship.

It was on understanding that this manager was extroverted (and understanding the ways in which extroverts typically act) that Gillian began to realise that because of the person's outgoing nature, she was just using her initiative and doing what she did best. It wasn't that she was trying to undermine her. She realised that she couldn't clip her team member's wings and needed to let her fly. Having this awareness enabled Gillian to adapt her approach with this manager and to develop a good working relationship.

BE AWARE OF YOUR OWN BIASES

We all have our own personal biases, and when we're not aware of them, it can cause us to treat others favourably whilst treating others less so. Sometimes we may not even be aware that those biases have shaped the decisions we have made and the impact this has then had on another person. Some people have unconscious biases on the basis of how they think other people view them, believing that they are being treated less favourably because of the other person's bias towards them. When we feel that we are under threat of an attack (as in this sort of situation), we often respond by putting up a defence, and by adopting a hostile approach to the person we perceive to be attacking us. For someone who holds an unconscious belief about a particular group of people, this could show itself in their body language, a lack of eye contact, or how you respond to them. It can also affect how you feel about your interactions with them, making you anxious about how you perform when you are with them.

Amy identified as being introverted and worked in an environment that was dominated by male extroverts. Whilst she knew that she was more than capable of doing the role, her biases towards extroverted men in her industry were hindering her progression without her realising it. Her defence barriers would go up, and she found it hard to relax and be herself. She was stereotyping that they were all the same. To those that didn't know her well she came across as stand-offish and impersonal when the real her was anything but. Helping her to become aware of her biases meant she was able to not let them influence how she responded in situations where she felt 'threatened'. This helped her to improve her working relationships and to be more impactful as a leader.

Do your defence barriers negatively affect your interactions? Have you ever stopped to think that you may have biases that are based on what you think other people's perceptions of you are? Getting to know people on a personal level and approaching encounters from a place of empathy as opposed to being judgemental will enable you to view situations differently and respond in ways that are not hostile. This will positively impact your interactions with these individuals.

Our biases can also play out in the way that we treat the people that we lead. Do you ever 'put upon' those who just get on and do it because it's easier than having to respond to the more challenging 'difficult' vocal person? Whilst that may be the easy option for you, how fair is it? How fair is it that because certain people are less vocal and don't complain, they're the ones who continuously get put up on, whereas their more vocal colleagues get left alone. Or there is the scenario where the more vocal ones get the attention and therefore get the opportunities – something that many introverts complain about.

Do you have any biases concerning any of your colleagues, client groups, stakeholders, or anyone else? Each and every day we make decisions based on our beliefs, understanding, assumptions and biases. If your role requires you to make decisions that involve people, how much are your decisions made on the basis of your biases, putting some at a disadvantage or some at an unfair advantage? Reflect back on decisions you have made in the past concerning people who didn't look like you, or were very dissimilar to you, and explore the reasoning behind your decisions. Then do the same thing again, but this time reflecting back on decisions you have made concerning people who were similar to you.

Don't let your personal biases hinder your leadership success.

BE ADAPTABLE TO CHANGE

I believe in lifelong learning and that leaders should constantly be developing themselves if they are to grow with changing times and remain relevant. If you are not embracing change and the changing face of the world of work, you will soon find yourself irrelevant. The pace of change happens so quickly these days and organisations are in a constant state of flux, with advancements in technology at the helm of our need to change and adapt.

The generation that are entering the workplace now have different expectations to those that entered 20 or even 10 years ago. They want flexibility. They want balance. They want to do meaningful work. They are prepared to go and find what they want elsewhere if they are not getting it where they are. Contrast this with how things were when I started work. It was not uncommon for people to start working at an organisation after leaving full-time education and to stay there for forty-plus years until they retired. Having too many jobs in a short space of time shown on your CV used to be frowned upon. Now when I look at the CVs of millennials, they are staying in jobs for a much shorter tenure. It's not uncommon for their CVs to show they've stayed one, maybe two years, at a job and moved on.

Artificial intelligence and machine learning are changing the landscape considerably. How prepared are you for an artificially intelligent future? As different ways of working come into place, different skills will gain significance. In 2016, the World Economic Forum listed the following as the top 10 skills needed to thrive in the fourth industrial revolution (the technological revolution):

- Complex problem solving
- Critical thinking
- Creativity
- People management
- Co-ordinating with others
- Emotional intelligence
- Judgement and decision making
- Service orientation
- Negotiation
- Cognitive flexibility

Qualities such as humility, adaptability, vision and constant engagement are likely to play a key role in the type of leadership that is required[12]. How do you fare when it comes to those skills and qualities?

There are many misconceptions about what humility is and people often think of someone who is humble as being passive and easy to walk over. Humility is actually a great strength to have, and the good thing is, as an introvert, you are more likely to be humble than if you were extroverted[13]. One study found that humility in

CEOs had a ripple effect of empowerment throughout the organisation[14]. Humble CEOs were positively associated with empowering behaviour, which in turn led to integrated top management teams, which in turn was more likely to mean that middle managers perceived that the climate of the organisation was empowering. This in turn meant there was more likely to be higher work engagement, a positive emotional connection to the organisation, and higher job performance.

Charisma, self-promotion, speaking up first and speaking the longest are often associated with being a competent leader, but do these attributes help to create inclusive environments? Apparently not. A study by the Catalyst Research Center found that qualities such as 'standing back', humility and self-sacrifice were more conducive to creating inclusive environments[15]. Some of the benefits of an inclusive work environment include higher employee retention, innovation, job satisfaction, improved performance and productivity, and in addition, it's also good for the bottom line.

To me, being humble is not something we shout about – it is something that is seen by others through our actions. Admitting when we are wrong, saying sorry when we have made a mistake, not hogging the limelight, letting others shine, showing others our appreciation, and expressing gratitude are all some of the things that help to keep us humble.

Become a lifelong learner and constantly develop yourself and stay up to date with changes and trends so that you are a creative and innovative leader, able to embrace and adapt to change, as well as being able to support those whom you lead through change.

BE ABLE TO FLEX WITH THE BEST OF THEM

As a leader you need to be able to adapt your style in certain situations. As an introverted leader, you may think that there is more of an expectation for you to act and behave more like your extroverted colleagues as opposed to it being vice versa. And yes, because of the unfavourable bias towards introverts, this is unfortunately so. We never hear people being told they need to think and reflect more, even though they would do well to do so.

Certain situations will require you to act in ways that feel contrary to your introverted nature and this is why self-awareness is so important. Not only so that you are aware that your default way of being may not get you the best outcome in a particular situation, but also so that you are aware of the effect different environments and situations have on your energy levels. That way you can factor in time to recharge so that you're not left with what I call introvert drain. The previous chapters provide you with tips and advice for ways in which you can adapt and still be your best in different situations and environments.

Not only is it good to have an awareness of how to adapt in different situations, but it also helps to know how to adapt when you are with different people in order to get the best out of them. Research by Anthony Grant and others found that introverts are better at managing teams of extroverts. The reason being that introverts typically don't like to hog the limelight and be centre of attention. As such, they let their extroverted team members run with their ideas[16]. Whereas with an extroverted leader, they and their extroverted team members are all competing for the limelight. They are all vying to be the centre of attention. Give your extroverted team members the freedom to be their extroverted selves, only reining them in where it is necessary for business or to let those less vocal be heard.

With your introverted team members, you may have to make more of an effort to engage with them. Unlike their extroverted colleagues, they are not necessarily going to be the ones always being vocal and being heard. Also, if you tend to retreat inwards and your introverted team members do too, you will have to make more of an effort to ensure that you communicate effectively and that your communications are heard and understood.

The same thing goes with managing different relationships. Whether it is your peers, those who are senior to you, stakeholders or customers, having an awareness of how you naturally are with different types of people will enable you to adapt your style in order to get the best out of your interactions with them. This is not about changing who you are, or about you putting on a different persona. It is about you being your authentic self and recognising that there will be times when you may need to be more vocal even if it feels uncomfortable. Or that you will have to 'socialise' in large groups making small talk even if this is painful. Or that you will have to give an on-the-spot response, even though your preferred way of being is to think and reflect first. Again, ways in which you can do these are described in previous chapters.

When it comes to stakeholders, colleagues and those more senior than you, developing good relationships will increase your ability to be influential and impactful. As a leader, you invariably get a lot of things done through other people. If you tend to be reserved, your natural way of being may be not to go out of your way to nurture these relationships because of the socialising and small talk that this may require. The chapter on networking will help to make this easier for you.

Because of the extrovert ideal that we have become so accustomed to[17], and the misconceptions that exist about introversion, you may find it challenging to be visible and to have the influence and impact you would like to have. Add to that any misconceptions or self-limiting beliefs that you hold about yourself, and it makes doing so even more challenging. Contrary to what many ill-informed people may think, introverts DO make great leaders. We only have to look at the likes of Michelle Obama, Hillary Clinton and Oprah Winfrey (all of whom are reported to be introverts).

I hope that what I have shared in this book will give

you plenty of food for thought and will help you to reflect on what you can do differently so that you lead with influence and impact. And not only that, but so that you are introvert and proud.

SELF-REFLECTION EXERCISE

- Now that you have come to the end of the book, what **WILL** you do differently, going forward?
- What, if anything, is likely to get in the way of you doing what you said you're going to do?
- What can you do to prevent this from happening?
- On a scale of 1 to 10 where 1 is you'll let this book gather dust on your bookshelf and 10 is 'I'm ready and raring to go!', where do you rate yourself in terms of confidence to do what you said you will do differently?
- If you rated yourself below an 8, what needs to happen to raise it by a point?
- If you rated yourself a 5 or below, what is the reason why you've not rated yourself a 6 (or a point higher if your rating was below a 5)?
- Whom can you ask to support you and hold you accountable with this?

Values Exercise

A TIME THAT YOU MOST ENJOYED

Think of a time in your career (or even in your personal life) that you most enjoyed – a time when you felt happy, content and fulfilled. What were you doing? What was present in your career/life at that time? What was it about what you were doing that was so important for you? Why did you enjoy it so much?

_____

_____

_____

_____

_____

A TIME THAT YOU LEAST ENJOYED

Think of a time in your career/life when you had to do something that you didn't enjoy and that left you feeling discontented and/or uncomfortable. What was it that you had to do? What was it about it that you did not enjoy? Why did you not enjoy doing it?

_____
_____
_____
_____
_____

Reflecting on your responses to the above and thinking about the things that are important to you and those that are not, what words or emotions come to mind? Tick the values from the list below that apply to you. If any of your values are not listed, enter them in the empty spaces, and continue on a separate sheet if needed.

Value	Value	Value	Value
Achievement	Authenticity	Adventure	Appreciation
Advancement	Authority	Ambition	Accountability
Autonomy	Acceptance	Abundance	Beauty
Balance	Belonging	Compassion	Courage
Challenge	Calmness	Control	Courtesy
Competitiveness	Community	Capability	Co-operation
Creativity	Cleanliness	Companionship	Decency
Dignity	Duty (sense of)	Development	Evolution
Equality	Encouragement	Enjoyment	Empathy
Education	Endurance	Experience	Friendship
Faith	Fairness	Freedom	Forgiveness
Fame	Faithfulness	Fun	Financial Freedom
Generosity	Grace	Gratitude	Growth
Humour	Health	Happiness	Honesty
Humility	Inner Strength	Innovation	Independence
Influence	Integrity	Joy	Justice
Learning	Knowledge	Kindness	Loyalty
Love	Leadership	Nurturing	Nature
Patience	Order	Openness	Obedience
Passion	Positivity	Peace (inner)	Professionalism
Purpose	Quality	Resourcefulness	Reliability
Respect	Responsibility	Recognition	Rationalisation
Realism	Serenity	Simplicity	Success
Solitude	Spirituality	Security	Support
Service	Stability	Tolerance	Trust
Truth	Uniqueness	Understanding	Virtue
Vision	Vitality	Variety	Wellbeing
Wisdom			

What are your top 5 values?

1.
2.
3.
4.
5.

How are these values reflected in your life?

_____

_____

_____

_____

How are these values reflected in your work?

_____

_____

_____

_____

What can you do to live in alignment with your values?

_____

_____

_____

_____

What values are important for you in your work life and why?

_____

_____

_____

_____

References

Introduction

1. The Myers Briggs description of ISTJ https://www.myersbriggs.org/my-mbti-personality-type/mbti-basics/the-16-mbti-types.htm?bhcp=1

Chapter One

1. Ross, P. (2017). If You're An Introvert, You're Probably Getting Screwed At Work. The Observer. [http://observer.com/2017/01/introverts-underrepresented-managerial-positions]
2. Vinnicombe, S., Sealy, R., Humbert, A. L. (2017). The Female FTSE Board Report 2017. https://www.cranfield.ac.uk/~/media/files/som-ftse-reports/cranfield-female-ftse-report-2017
3. Wikipedia description of intersectionality. https://en.wikipedia.org/wiki/Intersectionality
4. Stricker, L. J., Ross, J. (1964). An Assessment of Some Structural Properties of the Jungian Personality Typology. Journal of Abnormal and Social Psychology, 68(1), 62-71.

5. Oxford Reference defines cortical arousal as *'Activation of the reticular formation of the brain. Cortical arousal increases wakefulness, vigilance, muscle tone, heart rate, and minute ventilation'*. https://www.oxfordreference.com/view/10.1093/oi/authority.20110803095640881

6. Pervin, L., Cervone, D. (2010). *Personality: Theory and Research.* 11th ed., John Wiley And Sons, 2010, p. 251.

7. Morris, L. W. (1980). *Extraversion and Introversion: An Interactional Perspective p.5.* John Wiley & Sons Inc

8. Grimes, J. (2010). *Introversion And Autism: A Conceptual Exploration of The Placement of Introversion On the Autism Spectrum.* Electronic Theses and Dissertations. 4406. http://stars.library.ucf.edu/etd/4406

9. Lawn, R.B., Slemp, G.R., Vella-Brodrick, D.A. (2018). *Quiet Flourishing: The Authenticity and Well-Being of Trait Introverts Living in the West Depends on Extraversion-Deficit Beliefs.* Journal of Happiness Studies pp1-21 https://doi.org/10.1007/s10902-018-0037-5

10. Robson, D. (2017). *How East And West Think In Profoundly Different Ways.* BBC http://www.bbc.com/future/story/20170118-how-east-and-west-think-in-profoundly-different-ways

11. Pahwa, K. (2015). An Investigation of Key Personality Traits of Managers and Executives. University of Tennessee http://trace.tennessee.edu/utk_graddiss/3452

12. Recruitment and disability: online multiple-choice psychometric test was indirectly discriminatory (2017). XPert HR https://www.xperthr.co.uk/law-reports/recruitment-and-disability-online-multiple-choice-psychometric-test-was-indirectly-discriminatory/162106/

13. Stewart, C., Burdaky, S., (2017). *The Shy, the Brash and the Talkative.* The HR Director https://www.thehrdirector.com/product/single-issue-158/

14. Laney, M. O. (2002). *The Introvert Advantage: How Quiet People Can Thrive in an Extrovert World* pp. 27-28. New York: Workman Publishing

15. Ewen, R. B. (2014) *An Introduction to Theories of Personality 7th Edition* p376. Psychology Press

16. Spark, A., Stansmore, T., O'Connora, P. (2018). *The Failure of Introverts to Emerge as Leaders: The Role of Forecasted Affect.* Personality and Individual Differences 121 84–88

17. McHugh, A. S. (2017). *Introverts in The Church* p146. InterVarsity Press Books

Chapter 2

1. Ross, P. (2017). *If You're an Introvert, You're Probably Getting Screwed at Work.* The Observer https://observer.com/2017/01/introverts-underrepresented-managerial-positions/

2. Jacques-Hamilton, R., Sun, J., Smillie, L. (2018). *Costs and Benefits of Acting Extraverted: A Randomized Controlled Trial.* Journal of Experimental Psychology: General. American Psychological Association (APA) doi:10.1037/xge0000516.

3. Cain, S. (2013). *Quiet: The Power of Introverts in a World That Can't Stop Talking* p.4. Penguin Books

4. Ibarra, H. (2015). *The Authenticity Paradox: Why Feeling Like a Fake Can Be a Sign of Growth.* Harvard Business Review January-February 2015

5. McHugh, A. S. (2017). *Introverts in The Church.* InterVarsity Press Books

6. Lawn, B. R., Slemp, G., Vella-Brodrick, D. (2018). *Quiet Flourishing: The Authenticity and Well-Being of Trait*

Introverts Living in the West Depends on Extraversion-Deficit Beliefs. Journal of Happiness Studies. 10.1007/s10902-018-0037-5.

7. Palmer, S., Williams, H. (2012). Struggles with Low Self-Esteem: Teaching Self Acceptance. In Neenan, M., Palmer, S. (Eds.), *Cognitive Behavioural Coaching in Practice: An Evidence Based Approach* (pp.103-132). London: Routledge

8. Choi, Y., Iyengar, S. S., Ingram, P. (2017). *The Authenticity Challenge: How a Value Affirmation Exercise Can Engender Authentic Leadership.* Academy of Management Proceedings. 2017. 17318. 10.5465/AMBPP.2017.58.

9. "Character Strengths, Character Building Experts: VIA Character". *Viacharacter.Org,* 2019, Accessed From : http://bit.ly/2GxVNOJ

10. Crawley, C. (2017). *Ordinary Women Doing Extraordinary Things: 5 Steps to Add Extra to Ordinary p46.* 10-10-10 Publishing

Chapter 3

1. Corkindale, G (2008). *Overcoming Imposter Syndrome. Harvard Business Review,* https://hbr.org/2008/05/overcoming-imposter-syndrome

2. Cummins, D (2013). *Do You Feel Like an Imposter? Psychology Today.* https://www.psychologytoday.com/gb/blog/good-thinking/201310/do-you-feel-impostor

3. Clance, P. R., & Imes, S. A. (1978). *The Imposter Phenomenon in High Achieving Women: Dynamics and Therapeutic intervention.* Psychotherapy: Theory, Research & Practice, 15(3), 241-247. http://dx.doi.org/10.1037/h0086006

4. Cokley, K., McClain, S., Enciso, A.E., & Martinez, M.S. (2013). *An Examination of the Impact of Minority Status Stress and Impostor Feelings on the Mental Health of Diverse Ethnic Minority College Students.* Journal of Multicultural Counseling and Development 41(2), 82-95

5. Bryant A. (2010). *Good CEOs Are Insecure (and Know It).* New York Times https://www.nytimes.com/2010/10/10/business/10corner.html

6. Ali, H. (2019). *Her Way to The Top p75.* Panoma Press

7. Adapted from – Clance, P. R., & Imes, S. A. (1978). *The Imposter Phenomenon in High Achieving Women: Dynamics and Therapeutic Intervention.* Psychotherapy: Theory, Research & Practice, 15(3), 241-247. http://dx.doi.org/10.1037/h0086006

Chapter 4

1. Sandberg, S., Grant. A. (2015). *Opinion - Speaking While Female.* New York Times https://www.nytimes.com/2015/01/11/opinion/sunday/speaking-while-female.html.

2. Brescoll, V. L. (2011). *Who Takes The Floor And Why.* Administrative Science Quarterly, Vol 56, No. 4 pp. 622-641. *SAGE Publications,* doi:10.1177/0001839212439994.

3. Hvidsten, A. (2019) *Is Introversion An Obstacle In Tacit Knowledge Sharing Through Socialization? A Study On How Personality Traits Influence Knowledge Sharing Behavior.* Dalhousie Journal of Interdisciplinary Management https://ojs.library.dal.ca/djim/article/view/6442.

4. Goodwin, Charles. (1981). *Conversational Organization: Interaction Between Speakers and Hearers.* Academic Press

5. Ford, Cecilia E., and Trini Stickle. "Securing Recipiency In Workplace Meetings: Multimodal Practices". *Discourse Studies*, Vol 14, No. 1, 2012, pp. 11-30. *SAGE Publications*, doi:10.1177/1461445611427213.

6. Goodwin, Charles. (1981). *Conversational Organization: Interaction Between Speakers and Hearers.* Academic Press

7. Ravn, Ib. (2013). *A Folk Theory Of Meetings – And Beyond.* European Business Review 25(2) pp163-173 doi:10.1108/09555341311302666.

8. Lashinsky, A. (2012). Amazon's Jeff Bezos: The Ultimate Disrupter, http://fortune.com/2012/11/16/amazons-jeff-bezos-the-ultimate-disrupter/

Chapter 5

1. Goleman, D., Boyatzis, R., Davidson, R.J., Druskat, V., Kohlrieser, G. (2017). *Emotional Self-Awareness: A Primer (Building Blocks of Emotional Intelligence Book 1).* More Than Sound LLC.

2. Atamanik, C. (2013). *The Introverted Leader: Examining the Role of Personality and Environment.* Center for Leadership Current Research. 2. http://digitalcommons.fiu.edu/lead_research/2

3. NHS UK (2018). Breathing Exercise for Stress. https://www.nhs.uk/conditions/stress-anxiety-depression/ways-relieve-stress/

4. Rakal, D. (2018). *Learning Deep Breathing.* Psych Central Psych Central https://psychcentral.com/lib/learning-deep-breathing/

5. Bernstein E.S., Turban S. (2018). *The Impact of The 'Open' Workspace On Human Collaboration.* Phil. Trans. R. Soc. B 373: 20170239. http://dx.doi.org/10.1098/rstb.2017.0239

6. Oram, L. (2016). *A Method to My Quietness: A Grounded Theory Study of Living and Leading with Introversion.* (Electronic Thesis or Dissertation). Retrieved from https://etd.ohiolink.edu/
7. Laney, M. O. (2002). *The Introvert Advantage: How Quiet People Can Thrive in an Extrovert World.* New York: Workman Publishing p.255

Chapter 6

1. Stewart, C. (2016). *How Diverse is Your Pipeline? Developing the Talent Pipeline for Women and Black and Ethnic Minority Employees.* Industrial and Commercial Training, Vol. 48 No. 2, pp. 61-66
2. Greguletz, E., Diehl, M., Kreutzer, K. (2018). *Why Women Build Less Effective Networks Than Men: The Role of Structural Exclusion and Personal Hesitation.* Human Relations 001872671880430. 10.1177/0018726718804303.
3. Hewlett, S.A. (2011). *The Real Benefit of Finding a Sponsor.* Harvard Business Review https://hbr.org/2011/01/the-real-benefit-of-finding-a

Chapter 7

1. Bates, S. (2013). *The Science of Influence: The Three Dimensions of Executive Presence.* https://www.bates-communications.com/articles-and-newsletters/articles-and-newsletters/bid/57930/The-Science-of-Influence-The-Three-Dimensions-of-Executive-Presence
2. Hewlett, S.A., Leader-Chivée, L., Sherbin,L., Gordon, J., with Dieudonné, F. (2012).*Executive Presence – Key Findings.* https://www.talentinnovation.org/publication.cfm?publication=1340

3. Talley, L., Temple, S. (2015). *How Leaders Influence Followers Through the Use of Nonverbal Communication.* Leadership & Organization Development Journal, 36(1), 69-80.

4. Darioly, A., Mast, M. S. (2014). *The Role of Nonverbal Behavior In Leadership: An Integrative Review.* In R. E. Riggio & S. J. Tan (Eds.), *Leadership: Research and practice. Leader interpersonal and influence skills: The soft skills of leadership* (pp. 73-100). New York, NY, US: Routledge/Taylor & Francis Group.

5. Jensen, M. (2016). *Personality Traits and Nonverbal Communication Patterns.* International Journal of Social Science Studies. 4. 57-70. 10.11114/ijsss.v4i5.1451.

6. Kilduff, M., Mehra, A., Gioia, D. A., Borgatti, S. (2017). *Brokering Trust to Enhance Leadership: A Self-Monitoring Approach to Leadership Emergence.* 10.1007/978-3-319-45023-0_11.

7. Cain, S. (2013). *Quiet: The Power of Introverts In A World That Can't Stop Talking.* Penguin Books.

8. Little, B.R. (2014). *Me, Myself, and Us: The Science of Personality and the Art of Well-Being.* Public Affairs™.

9. Author Brian Little on Personality and the 'Art of Well-being'. (2015). accessed from https://knowledge.wharton.upenn.edu/article/the-science-of-personality-understanding-yourself-and-those-around-you/

10. Amy Cuddy Ted Talk Your Body Language May Shape Who You Are (2012) http://www.ted.com/talks/amy_cuddy_your_body_language_shapes_who_you_are

11. Cuddy, A. J. C., Schultz, J., Fosse, N.E. (2018). *P-Curving a More Comprehensive Body of Research on Postural Feedback Reveals Clear Evidential Value For Power-Posing Effects: Reply to Simmons and Simonsohn (2017).* Psychological Science. 29. 095679761774674. 10.1177/0956797617746749.

12. Schumann, K., Ross, M. (2010). *Why Women Apologize More Than Men: Gender Differences in Thresholds for Perceiving Offensive Behavior.* Psychological science. 21. 1649-55. 10.1177/0956797610384150.

13. Lerner, H. (2015). *Why Women Over-Apologize: How and Why To Stop It!* Psychology Today https://www.psychologytoday.com/gb/blog/the-dance-connection/201511/why-women-over-apologize-how-and-why-stop-it

14. Oram, L. (2016). *A Method to My Quietness: A Grounded Theory Study of Living and Leading with Introversion.* (Electronic Thesis or Dissertation). Retrieved from https://etd.ohiolink.edu/

15. BI Norwegian Business School. (2013). *Intuition, analytical skills matter most in crisis.* Retrieved July 4, 2019 from https://www.bi.edu/research/business-review/articles/2013/12/intuition-and-analytical-skills-matter-most-in-a-crisis/

Chapter 8

1. Humphrey, R. H. (2002). *The Many Faces of Emotional Leadership.* The Leadership Quarterly, 13(5), 493–504

2. Goleman, D., Boyatzis, R., Senge, P., Druskat, V., Lippincott, M., Taylor, M. (2017). *Influence: A Primer (Building Blocks of Emotional Intelligence Book 8).* More Than Sound.

3. Vergauwe, J., Wille, B., Hofmans, J., Kaiser, R., De Fruyt, F. (2017). *The Double-Edged Sword of Leader Charisma: Understanding the Curvilinear Relationship Between Charismatic Personality and Leader Effectiveness.* Journal of Personality and Social Psychology. 114. 10.1037/pspp0000147.

4. Goleman, D., Boyatzis, R., Davidson, R.J., Druskat, V., Kohlrieser, G. (2017). *Emotional Self-Awareness: A Primer (Building Blocks of Emotional Intelligence Book 1)*. More Than Sound.

5. Duffy, K., Chartrand, T.L. (2015). *The Extravert Advantage: How and When Extraverts Build Rapport With Other People*. Psychological science. 26. 10.1177/0956797615600890.

6. Carey, B. (2008). *You Remind Me of Me*. New York Times https://www.nytimes.com/2008/02/12/health/12mimic.html

7. Guéguen, Nicolas & Jacob, Céline & Martin, Angelique. (2009). *Mimicry in Social Interaction: Its Effect on Human Judgment and Behavior*. European Journal of Social Sciences – Volume Number. 8.

8. Ames, D.R., Benjamin, L.B, Brockner, J. (2012). *The Role of Listening in Interpersonal Influence*. Journal of Research in Personality 46. 345–349. 10.1016/j.jrp.2012.01.010.

9. Lee, D., Hatesohl, D. (1993). *Listening: Our Most Used Communication Skill. Extension*. University of Missouri http://extension.missouri.edu/p/CM150

10. Kaufman, B. (2011). *Leadership Strategies: Build Your Sphere of Influence*. Business Strategy Series. 12(6). 315-320. 10.1108/17515631111185950.

11. Goleman, D., Boyatzis, R., Davidson, R.J., Druskat, V., Kohlrieser, G. (2017). *Empathy: A Primer (Building Blocks of Emotional Intelligence Book 6)*. More Than Sound.

12. Goleman, D. (2007). *Three Kinds of Empathy - Cognitive, Emotional, Compassionate*. http://www.danielgoleman.info/three-kinds-of-empathy-cognitive-emotional-compassionate/

13. Goleman, D. (2011). *Social Intelligence: The New Science of Human Relationships* p191. Cornerstone Digital.

14. Goleman, D. (2011). *Social Intelligence: The New Science of Human Relationships* p159. Cornerstone Digital.

15. Goleman, D. (2006). *Emotional Intelligence: Why it Can Matter More than IQ* p146. Bantam Books.

16. Zeffane, R., Tipu, S., Ryan, J. (2011). *Communication, Commitment & Trust: Exploring the Triad.* International Journal of Business and Management. 6. 10.5539/ijbm.v6n6p77.

17. Pink, D. H. (2013). *To Sell Is Human: The Surprising Truth About Persuading, Convincing and Influencing Others.* Canongate Books.

18. Dent, F. E. (2010). *Influencing – The Skill for Success.* Ashridge Business School http://tools.ashridge.org.uk/website/IC.nsf/wFARATT/Influencing%20-%20the%20skill%20for%20success/$file/InfluencingTheSkillForSuccess.pdf

19. Tartakovsky, M. (2018). *5 Tips to Increase Your Assertiveness.* Psych Central https://psychcentral.com/lib/5-tips-to-increase-your-assertiveness/.

20. Paterson, R.J. (2000). *The Assertiveness Workbook: How to Express Your Ideas and Stand Up for Yourself at Work and in Relationships.* New Harbinger Publications.

Chapter 9

1. Gandolfi, F., Stone, S. (2016). *Clarifying Leadership: High-impact Leaders in a Time of Leadership Crisis.* Review of International Comparative Management 17(3)

2. Passmore, J. (2015). *Leadership Coaching: Working with Leaders to Develop Elite Performance 2nd Edition* p6. Kogan Page.

3. Kouzes, J.M., Posner, B.Z. (2012). *The Leadership Challenge: How to Make Extraordinary Things Happen in Organizations 5th edition* p.115. Jossey-Bass, A Wiley Imprint

4. Kouzes, J.M., Posner, B.Z. (2012). *The Leadership Challenge: How to Make Extraordinary Things Happen in Organizations 5th edition* p.113. Jossey-Bass, A Wiley Imprint

5. Adair, J. (2011). *Effective Leadership: How to Be a Successful Leader.* Pan

6. Carton, A. M., Lucas, B. J. (2018). *How Can Leaders Overcome the Blurry Vision Bias? Identifying an Antidote to the Paradox of Vision Communication.* Academy of Management Journal 2018, Vol. 61, No. 6, 2106–2129. https://doi.org/10.5465/amj.2015.0375

7. Gandolfi, F., Stone, S. (2016). *Clarifying Leadership: High-impact Leaders in a Time of Leadership Crisis.* Review of International Comparative Management 17(3)

8. Goleman, D., Boyatzis, R. E. (2017). *Emotional Intelligence Has 12 Elements.* Which Do You Need to Work On? Harvard Business Review https://hbr.org/2017/02/emotional-intelligence-has-12-elements-which-do-you-need-to-work-on

9. Gandolfi, F., Stone, S. (2016*). Clarifying Leadership: High-impact Leaders in a Time of Leadership Crisis.* Review of International Comparative Management 17(3)

10. Laney, M. O. (2002). *The Introvert Advantage: How Quiet People Can Thrive in an Extrovert World* p215. New York: Workman Publishing

11. Thomas, M. (2015). *Your Late Night Emails are Hurting Your Team.* Harvard Business Review https://hbr.

org/2015/03/your-late-night-emails-are-hurting-your-team

12. Gray, A. (2016). *The 10 Skills You Need to Thrive in the Fourth Industrial Revolution.* World Economic Forum https://www.weforum.org/agenda/2016/01/the-10-skills-you-need-to-thrive-in-the-fourth-industrial-revolution/

13. O'Connor, P., Spark, A. (2017). *Introverts Are Often Reluctant to Lead — But That Doesn't Mean They Aren't Capable.* ABC https://www.abc.net.au/news/2017-09-26/introverts-are-reluctant-leaders-but-they-are-capable/8988250

14. Atamanik, C.(2013). *The Introverted Leader: Examining the Role of Personality and Environment.* Center for Leadership Current Research. 2. http://digitalcommons.fiu.edu/lead_research/2

15. Prime, J., Salib, E.R. (2014). *Inclusive Leadership: The View From Six Countries.* Catalyst https://www.catalyst.org/research/inclusive-leadership-the-view-from-six-countries/

16. Grant, A. M., Francesca, G., Hofmann, D. (2011). *Reversing the Extraverted Leadership Advantage: The Role of Employee Proactivity.* Academy of Management Journal. 54. 528-550. 10.5465/AMJ.2011.61968043

17. Cain, S. (2013). *Quiet: The Power of Introverts In a World That Can't Stop Talking* p4. Penguin Books

CPSIA information can be obtained
at www.ICGtesting.com
Printed in the USA
LVHW051311241120
672562LV00013B/249

9 781913 192693